D1126682

Successful Management Information Systems

Research for Business Decisions, No. 78

Richard N. Farmer, Series Editor

Professor of International Business
Indiana University

Other Titles in This Series

Successful Management Information Systems

Revised Edition

by
Helen H. Ligon

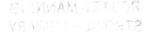

UMI RESEARCH PRESS
Ann Arbor, Michigan

Sc,
T
58.6
L54
1986

Copyright © 1986, 1978
Helen Hailey Ligon
All rights reserved

Produced and distributed by
UMI Research Press
an imprint of
University Microfilms, Inc.
Ann Arbor, Michigan 48106

Library of Congress Cataloging in Publication Data

Ligon, Helen H. (Helen Hailey), 1921-
  Successful management information systems.

  (Research for business decisions ; no. 78)
  "A revision of author's Ph. D. thesis, Texas A & M,
1976"—T.p. verso.
    Bibliography: p.
    Includes index.
    1. Management information systems.   I. Title.
II. Series.
T58.6.L54   1986   658.4'038   86-6979
ISBN 0-8357-1703-8 (alk. paper)

ROBERT MANNING
STROZIER LIBRARY

MAR 12 1987

Tallahassee, Florida

Contents

List of Tables

viii *List of Tables*

1

Introduction

"The Information Age" is a label given to the 1980s by journalists and academicians alike. In keeping with this theme, the idea of using information as a competitive weapon has gained much credence and popularity. Successful business operations both large and small have depended on information as a vital component. In a speech to the Society for Information Management in October 1984, Warren McFadden outlined the ways companies such as American Airlines and the American Hospital Association had attained competitive advantages over their competition by using computerized information [126].

Communication improvement, newer production methods, and the growth of computer technology and understanding have all caused companies to demand more and more information. As society has become more complex and as the sheer volume of information has exploded, both businesses and government have increasingly required more relevant information on a timely basis. To the forefront of business requirements has come a greater emphasis on having information more quickly available.

The pressures of the 1980s that give impetus to the demand for quicker information include the enormous size of business operations today, the myriad complexities involved in such organizations, and the multitude of people necessary for successful achievement of company objectives. The advent of the computer and its potential for assisting in making the necessary information available have necessitated the attempt to develop information systems for these large, diversified, and complex organizations.

Designing a large-scale management information system (MIS) is not a new problem; it is not something management has just recently recognized as being essential. However, until the possibility of using computers to assist in information acquisition came to fruition, managers placed much more emphasis on such problems as achieving efficient production or maximizing the use of financial resources. In the 1970s, many large-scale information systems simply evolved without extensive planning or without any set pattern of development. Robert Murdick and Joel Ross stated that "the production of information is at least as important as the production of physical commodities." They further added: "The now-expanding discipline of management information systems regards information as a resource equal in importance to the traditional ones of men, money, materials, and machines" [136:239]. In the 1980s their ideas have been accepted and have been carried one step further—information is as important as the traditional four M's, and furthermore, information *can* be managed.

Study of Conceptual Design

Certainly a business is more competitive with a successful information system. In the previously mentioned speech, Warren McFarland suggested three periods in the development of computer usage:

1. Computer technology played a useful backup role in the 1970s.

2. For others, the backup tool became an "avenging weapon," allowing pricing strategies and opportunity to drive their competitors into bankruptcy.

3. In 1984 and in the near future, coordinated integration of large-scale data processing and telecommunication will make the "weapon." [126]

Murdick and Ross wrote that in the late 1970s "no other field offers such concentrated room for improvement as do information analysis and the design of information systems for decision making" [136:239]. For that time frame, no set pattern for the analysis and design of large-scale information systems existed. Reams of literature, much of it contradictory, marked the thinking about design concepts for information systems. A study of these writings, however, revealed that the majority of the articles or books of the 1970s were either "cookbook type" (how to do it), or were vague generalized ideas. At that time, a gap seemed to exist in both the literature and in practice because these were emerging concepts, not yet highly structured or finalized.

The author's original research proposed to construct a set of guidelines applicable to designing a management information system. An extensive search was made of the applicable literature, with emphasis on pertinent characteristics influencing success or failure. To management in the 1970s and currently, the design of information systems has become a vital and critical ingredient for successful business operations. Originally, selected guidelines were developed so that companies could follow them in establishing or improving their management information system.

During the time period between publication of the first edition and the present edition, numerous successful management information systems have been developed. At the time of the first writing, only a few "successful" systems existed. Three of the then-successful systems (American Airlines, AT&T, and Weyerhaeuser) were studied and compared to the guidelines. How do the current management information systems compare to these guidelines? Later chapters in this book address this question, as the three original companies are brought into the 1980s.

Applicable Definitions

"Data" were defined in my 1978 study as facts and figures not currently being used in a decision process. In contrast, "information" referred to the classified or interpreted data being used for decision making.

Although no consensus has been reached on an adequate definition of a management information system, characteristics from two definitions were the basis for the findings of this research. Gordon B. Davis of the University of Minnesota defines the MIS as "an information system that, in addition to providing all necessary transaction processing for an organization provides information and processing support for management and decision functions. The idea of such an information system preceded the advent of the computers, but computers made the idea feasible"[57:vii]. A more thorough definition is that of Walter J. Kennevan. Although Kennevan's definition was created in 1970, the ideas are completely applicable to the 1980s. He defined the MIS as "an organized method of providing past, present, and projection information relating to internal operations and external intelligence. It supports the planning, control, and operational functions of an organization by furnishing uniform information in the proper time frame to assist the decision-making process"[108:63].

Another lucid, but more condensed definition seemed briefly to present the essence of a management information system. J. D. Aron stated that a MIS was an "information system that provides the manager with *that* information he needs to make decisions" [12:233]. Aron's definition is more in keeping with the current idea of decision support systems.

By "large-scale" information systems, this writer refers to those systems which are computer-based, process voluminous amounts of data, consolidates these data, and makes the condensations available to managers for decision-making purposes.

Proposed Objectives and Related Methodology

First, this study chronologically traces the evolution of data processing in business, with emphasis on information handling for decision making. The present edition brings in newer concepts such as information centers, micro-computers, spreadsheets, workbenches, automated design tools, structured design, fourth-generation languages, and prototyping.

The examination was conducted through a search of pertinent literature related to changing management methods for recording and utilizing business information. Data bases and their current applications are also included in this edition.

A second objective is to evaluate analytically the changes in concepts toward management methods for obtaining information. To meet this objective, the methodology entailed a literature search. However, more emphasis is given to "how" and "why" management concepts have changed. After the "total" concept is discussed, emphasis is given to the interest-disillusionment syndrome that businesses experience after becoming disen-chanted with the "total" systems approach. Richard Nolan's classic, "Stages of Growth," is related to current practices and updated to include current thinking. Contemporary concepts about information systems are also eval-uated, with a discussion of possible reasons for their evolution.

Next, we compiled a consensus of the ideas of well-known writers and practitioners in the information systems field. In the original study, particu-lar attention was given to the design concepts applicable to these phases of the systems development life cycle:

1. Feasibility study

2. Requirements analysis

3. Systems specifications

4. Systems design

5. Coding and programming

6. Testing

7. Documentation

8. Implementation

Findings are presented as of 1978, when the first research study was com-pleted.

With these same steps as the basis of analysis and design, a follow-up has been made to determine how thinking has changed as more experience has been gained in developing successful information systems. From writings of both academicians and businessmen in the MIS field, we selected a set of criteria which forced better design planning. The original set of criteria was a composite of the thinking of recognized, well-known experts in the MIS field. Such criteria have been updated to reflect current ideas concerning MIS development.

The Delphi technique was used in the original study to determine whether the criteria obtained from the literature search were "reasonably likely," in statistical terminology. Through the Delphi method, a composite of experts in the information system field was questioned. Included in this group were both well-known business authorities and accomplished writers. The Delphi method was used to determine whether or not these experts agreed or disagreed as to the "reasonableness" of the criteria developed through the literature search. Details of the Delphi questionnaires are presented in the Appendix.

In 1984, the Delphi was "revisited," i.e., the same survey was sent to the original participants and then enlarged to include other people prominent in the MIS field. A comparison and a contrast was made of the thinking of these experts, as more and more successful management information systems have been developed.

Originally, the Bell Telephone System's BISCUS/FACS (Business Information System Customer Service/Facilities Customer Service) System was examined in a field study. During this study, particular attention was given to Bell's problems and progress in implementing BISCUS/FACS. Criteria obtained from both the literature search and the Delphi Study were applied to that system for comparison. As part of this examination, interviews were held with Bell employees who worked on the proposed BIS (Business Information System) and who converted the Dallas office to BISCUS/FACS in 1975.

In 1982, the Bell System was separated into independent operating companies, one of which was Southwestern Bell Telephone Company. Where BISCUS/FACS has gone since the 1975 implementation was discussed with employees at the Dallas office. How divestiture has affected the flow of information within the Bell system and how this original information system has evolved were also discussed.

Originally the American Airlines' SABRE system and the Weyerhaeuser Company's information system were examined, with the criteria as guidelines. Much information about these two companies came from published literature concerning the two systems, since their successes have been well documented. In addition, involved personnel from both companies discussed the development of their management information systems with the author. Again, criteria obtained from the research were applied to the systems for comparison.

American Airlines is one of the companies that has been heralded as using its information system to gain and maintain a comparative advantage. Since deregulation of the airline industry, the company has been harassed for the manner in which it has used its system. Discussion of both the pros and cons of usage of such a system are presented.

Finally, all of the above-listed information was applied in the original study to conclusively test the hypothesis that large-scale information systems *do* possess certain common characteristics for the conceptual design phase. A subhypothesis was that these characteristics were related to the success of such systems. The culminating evaluation applied characteristics found in the various systems either to refute the hypothesis or to give credence to the belief that common characteristics for successful systems existed and could be delineated.

A study of literature published since the original book was written verifies the truth of the hypothesis. Out of the developmental work on management information systems has come an almost-universal set of common characteristics. Guidelines for the development of such systems have been created by several of the major accounting firms doing consulting work for large firms. Current literature verifies that guidelines have been developed and are working in successful information systems. What was once a mystique has since become something that can be developed and taught.

The original study developed an emerging pattern of selected guidelines useful to a company planning to install a management information system. How these guidelines apply to systems developed in the 1980s is discussed in this edition. Current technology and advances in computer usage, especially with micros, are other valuable developments detailed here. Features that are desirable and factors to be avoided are also outlined in this study.

2

Evolution of Data Processing in Business

Change is a way of life in commercial organizations. Similarly, since the advent of the computer, organizational concepts toward information gathering and utilization have also changed. This book chronicles such concepts from the late 1950s through the middle 1980s, with emphasis on computer utilization in handling business information.

Early Business Data Processing

Any chronology of computer usage in business may begin with the idea that records were an important facet of business survival even before the computer arrived on the scene. Consequently, small businesses usually had simple records, with much of the vital business information being maintained in the the mind of the owner rather than in an accessible, readable form.

From the inception of business, information has been an essential element — some call it the lifeblood of an organization. As George Steiner stated, "Information flows are as important to the life and health of a business as the flow of blood is to the life and health of an individual [182]."

People lived on earth for many centuries before they felt the necessity for keeping records. However, development of trade and commerce along with the growth of cities brought the need for more details coupled with a system for recording these details. Early in the life cycle of business, some method of collecting necessary information was undertaken. First efforts to obtain information entailed no particular method of data collection. With the passage of time, however, a systematic, orderly method of collecting vital information evolved. One of the earliest examples of record keeping was that of the Chinese. By the 1400s, Venetian business owners, managers, and financiers all utilized Pacioli's double-entry system of recording business information for future references. In discussing other early innovative manual record-keeping techniques, Donald Sanders also listed the record audits of the Greeks and the banking systems and budgets of the Romans [167].

In the twenty years following the Civil War, manual methods were the predominant techniques for data recording in the United States. Clerks were the data processors and their tools included pencils, rulers, worksheets, journals, and ledgers. As Sanders stated, "Such complete reliance upon manual methods resulted, of course, in information which was relatively inaccurate and often late" [167].

Punched Card Applications

The 1890 census brought a major milestone in record keeping. Dr. Herman Hollerith devised punched card equipment for expediting the counting of the census so that the enumeration could be completed before the time for the next census. Gradually these same machines were utilized in business since companies had the same problem as the census bureau — the rudimentary system that worked for small operations "got tired and careless under high volume conditions. And during the next 40 years volume was to become the byword of American industry" [167].

Computer Technology Applied to Business

No revolutionary changes were evident in information collection and dissemination until the advent of computers. Their introduction into the business world called for changes in information-keeping methods. However, the first applications of computers in business were no more than the manual methods converted "as is" to computer processing. In most instances, very minor changes were made in the method of record keeping as companies merely put their current manual record system in computerized form.

Initially, when the unit-record methods were converted to computerized ones, programming was simple. The problems involved with programming, along with the "state of the art" during this period of time, influenced many businesses to avoid making drastic changes in their information-keeping methods. Robert Head remarked that "even if efficient, high capacity random access storage had been available . . . it is doubtful whether it could have been exploited very effectively given the kinds of applications then being converted to computers" [87]. In two of his books, Donald Sanders referred to this era as the "Victorian Period" [165, 167]. R. George Glaser epitomized this period in his statement that "these routine applications could be justified economically by relatively straightforward extensions of known cost factors, and apart from some procedural adjustments, little in the company had to change" [76].

Commercial applications then branched into more sophisticated usage, but all of these were considered to be separate or isolated methods. According to Cyrus Gibson and Richard Nolan, this stage of growth was principally marked by a proliferation of applications in all of the functional areas of business [73]. A 1958 article in *The Franklin Institute Journal* described the use of the computer for repetitive business operations [98]. In 1958, C. S. Knox emphasized how the computer could simplify purchase decisions [112], while a paper in the *Oil and Gas Journal* from this same year enumerated ways in which computers worked on "tough problems for Socony's world-wide operations" [47].

A majority of the computer articles in this time period described either scientific, engineering, statistical, or operations research applications, such as production control, product design, or simulations [9, 58, 65, 112, 113, 138, 149, 151]. In a discussion about this era, Glaser commented that "the next era of computer applications saw the rise of business systems for inventory control, production scheduling, cash management, and the like. At the time these applications were designed and implemented they were considered to be very complex" [76]. In a slightly different vein, a 1957 article proclaimed that the computer was a "new giant brain for business-men" [67], while a 1958 discussion portrayed the computer as an aid in economic studies [65].

Indicative of either reluctance to accept the computer as a major catalyst for change or to recognize the impact the computer was having on business operation and organization, is the manner in which the technical indices handled this new technology. Although the first computer acquired for business data processing was installed at General Electric's Appliance Park in Louisville, Kentucky in 1954, not until the 1965 issue of *Applied Science and Technology Index* were computers listed as a separate category. Prior to 1965, computers were listed under "calculating machines," with only a cross-reference under the title "computer."

After World War II, many of the wartime methods and discoveries used to solve battlefield and supply problems were applied to business. Also, there was an increase in control theory work during the war, with a number of leaders emerging from Hughes Aircraft Company. In a discussion of scientific discoveries and technological changes accelerated because of wartime need, Sanders remarked that "peaceful application of defense-inspired discoveries have resulted in new commercial materials and products" [167]. Included in these products were computers.

As businesses expanded in size, complexity, and financial worth, and as knowledge of computers and their utilization increased, some companies began to select particular aspects of their businesses for conversion to computerization. For example, numerous companies felt that computers would greatly facilitate inventory control. Therefore, the inventory process was analyzed and then adapted to computerization.

Evolution of the Systems Concept

During this era, one of the evolving methods adopted by businesses was the "systems" idea. Combination of the system method with use of computers meant that the more progressive businesses seriously considered integration of previously separate computer applications. Instead of just converting manual processes then in use, several companies instigated studies of inventory methods, looking toward ways of possible improvement. Thus evolved the idea of an inventory "system." Wherever computer programs used the same source of data, attempts were made to combine these programs in order to eliminate both redundancy and unnecessary costs. Glaser discussed another problem faced by firms attempting the systems approach: "Significantly, companies began to realize that these more complex systems could raise sticky issues of corporate policy. . . . It became apparent that computer systems were introducing a new dimension of difficulty." [76].

"Total" Systems

In the 1950s there appeared a movement toward the theoretical idea of the "total" system. Much of the literature of this era extolled the virtue of an integrated system which combined all the elements of a business. Such a system would conceivably make needed information available to all management personnel. On paper, this concept sounded like the answer to all business problems. Having such information available for any business decision in a timely manner and in the form desired is indeed an ideal. The major drawback in bringing this idea to fruition in the 1950s was the "state of the art" of both computer hardware and software of that period.

Literature between 1958 and 1961 contained the term "data processing systems," but such references were really to problem solving or information gathering and reporting. The context in which the term "system" was utilized did not appear to be in a truly integrated sense. A 1958 article in *Gas Age* had the enticing title, "Total Data Processing May Number Days of the Punched Card as a Business Document" [99]. Perusal of this article, however, revealed that the term "total" as used in the article did not in any way relate to the idea of integrating business information into a unified whole. D. L. Aswen also included the term in an article in which he described an automatic data collection system [15].

The 1960s brought decreased cost of hardware and improvements in software and made a "total" system appear to be feasible. Since the "total" system concept was in vogue in the 1960s, many companies attempted to bring such a concept to fruition [65, 67, 72, 81, 83, 93, 128]. By 1961, the "systems" concept began to creep into literature listings, with the term "total" appearing in the following title: "Total Analysis Digital System for Chromatographs" [104]. Evidence of the changing attitude toward computer utilization was revealed by the title "New Information Systems," which appeared in the August 1961 issue of *The Franklin Institute Journal* [93]. In 1963 a similar article appearing in *The Journal of Petroleum Technology* had the title "Information Retrieval: A Valuable Tool or Costly Waste?" [157]; and a 1964 article by J. Moss discussed methods of "Planning a Management Information System" [134].

By 1964, the terms "total systems" and "integrated systems" appeared in numerous literature listings. One such article was in *Canadian Chemical Processing* and was entitled: "Total MIS: How It Is Achieved" [190]. Describing the atmosphere prevailing in 1964, Russell L. Ackoff commented, "Enthusiasm for such systems is understandable; it involves the researcher in a romantic relationship with the most glamorous instrument of our time, the computer" [2].

The concept of a "total" system was a dream, an ideal. Implementation, on the other hand, was difficult and utilized only in limited situations. Selected companies like those in life insurance, banking, and industrial manufacturing recognized the need for changes. As A. W. Smith stated in his 1966 article from *Administrative Management*, "Practically all companies recognize that a 'total system' is vital to long range programs" [176].

Disillusionment with MIS

As with many dreams, the dream of a "total" information system did not materialize. In a 1967 article, Glaser vividly described the prevailing situation. "Management information systems (especially the "total" or "integrated" variety) are currently much in vogue. . . . Of course, only a few zealots would seek to realize this objective literally. More practically systems designers realize that it would be technically impossibly and economically untenable to collect *all* the relevant data" [76]. Storage costs were still too high for any but the largest corporations to afford. Furthermore, even though great advances had been made in hardware, gaps still existed for those who dreamed of a "total" information system.

Among reasons why such a concept did not work were these:

1. Mass storage devices were slow and very expensive [55, 165, 144].

2. Operating systems and software, such as data base management systems, were not yet operational or perfected [2, 90, 169].

3. Numerous problems of size existed because the "total" system concept involved such a massive amount of information [157, 198].

4. Human adaptation presented serious problems [198, 206].

In a 1967 article entitled "Management Misinformation Systems," Russell L. Ackoff stated, "Contrary to the impression produced by the growing literature, few computerized management information systems have been put into operation . . . most have not matched expectations, and *some* have been outright failures" [2]. As late as 1971, Edward Tolliver, in the article, "Myths of Automated Management Systems," reported, "To date computers have generally discouraged really major changes in management processes by making it economically feasible to continue doing things the old way. And, once the old way is automated, change becomes more difficult and expensive" [188].

In spite of these reports, several attempts during this period were quite close to the "total systems" dream. Two of these, which will be analyzed, are the Weyerhaeuser Company application [41], and SABRE, the American Airlines reservation system [116, 117, 164]. The true status during this era was vividly portrayed in Glaser's statement that "a tremendous gap exists between what is theoretically possible and what is operationally and economically feasible" [76].

The 1970s brought still lower hardware costs coupled with the initiation of special languages for handling data bases. Along with such innovations, the possibility of some aspect of integrated systems seemed to exist. Costs were still a problem; software still did not seem as reliable as desired. Yet, on a small scale, many organizations began working toward an integrated method of storing information and of being able to retrieve this information when needed.

Very seldom did literature of this period contain a chronicle of failure, since people do not often write about their failures. However, according to several 1972 articles, failures were reported at United Airlines and TWA [80]. Also, after spending large sums of money in an attempt to implement a "total" system, American Telephone and Telegraph Company backed off from this concept to try less ambitious projects [185, 198, 205].

Because the idea of the "total" system was years in advance of both hardware and software capabilities, many companies were forced to retreat to the modular (or subsystem) approach. Two articles discussed such disillusionment in presenting what computers can and cannot do [144, 200]. Glaser explained that the typical approach of this time period was "to integrate certain closely related functions of the business—inventory control and production scheduling in a manufacturing company, for example" [76].

BIS in the Bell System

Donald R. Woodford, managing editor of the *Bell Telephone Magazine*, discussed the introduction of BIS (Business Information System) into the Bell Telephone Company by stating that "in all respects, the concepts of a business information system is an inevitable product of the age" [205]. In 1968, G. N. Thayer wrote an article which discussed BIS and explained that its goal was to manage the flow of business information more effectively [185]. The same paper described a joint study made by AT&T and Bell Labs in the mid-1950s on the use of computers for commercial applications. Although the study was discontinued in 1958, the results laid the groundwork for Bell's first computerized billing system. According to Thayer, this study was "to become a key transitional step toward a modern business information system."

Realizing that a completely integrated BIS would be too massively complex and costly for any one operating company to develop alone, AT&T formed a planning group. The purpose of this group was to study possibilities in twelve major operating areas: billing and collecting, service order processing, disbursement accounting, personnel records, equipment ordering, supply operations, directory operations, outside plant engineering, trunk-facilities estimating, trunk-facilities engineering, trunk-facilities administration, and construction program administration.

Stages of Electronic Data Processing (EDP) Development Summarized

In little more than twenty-five years, the computer has advanced from an expensive luxury to a cost-justifiable necessity. Hugh Watson and Archie Carroll stated that "the primary reason computers have experienced such tremendous growth can be summed up in one word—applications" [195]. These applications, or potential applications, have been increasing at such a rapid pace that it is mind-boggling. Currently, the trend is toward such innovative concepts as the use of minicomputers, distributive processing, increasing timesharing, computer networks, data bases, and computer utilities—all with microcomputers as part of the link.

Not only have computers affected and influenced the way data have been processed and information disseminated, but they also have had a profound influence on the business organizational hierarchy itself. Robert Head has stated that "from its earliest beginning, penetration by the computer into the business organization has affected people. . . . Gradually, as experience was gained and the unique abilities of the computer became better understood, the impact of computers on company personnel began to extend upward" [87].

An explicit and precise summary of the evolution of computer usage in business was compiled by Gibson and Nolan in two separate articles. Ideas from the two articles, each containing a similar growth and development curve, have been consolidated into the one curve presented in figure 1. This combined graph has been given the title from a 1973 article by Gibson and Nolan: "The Stages of EDP Development" [73, 74].

This summary follows the pattern described in this chapter. An initiation period came first, with cost-reduction accounting applications such as payroll, accounts receivable, accounts payable, and billing. Proliferation of applications in all the functional areas comprised the second stage. The third phase was epitomized by a moratorium on new applications and emphasis on control. For a majority of companies, stage four is in the future, since the emphasis or main focus characterizing this stage is data base applications. According to Gibson and Nolan, "Currently some large companies have reached the tail-end of the S-shaped EDP budget curve: their departments are mature. . . . One thing certain is that computer technology advancements are continuing at an unrelenting pace" [73].

Stages of EDP Development Extending into the 1980s

In 1979, Richard L. Nolan presented two more stages in the growth of data processing. Stage V was labeled "Data administration," with "Maturity" being the label on Stage VI. During the data administration phase, Nolan suggested that data would be shared and that common systems would be developed along with increased data administration by the DP organization. Also during the fifth stage, Nolan stated that there would be more user awareness calling for effective accountability of the DP department. The "Maturity" stage presented for the first time the concept of data as a resource which should be managed. To manage this valuable resource, Nolan noted the need for strategic planning. Again, users were included under the idea of joint user and data processing accountability for the accuracy and effectiveness of data.

The New Job of The Data Manager

Leading into the 1980s, Nolan's article presented an innovative idea that the job of "data manager" could become a vital and even necessary position in efficient data processing shops. Forest Horton, Jr. (*Journal of Systems*

Figure 1. The Stages of EDP Development

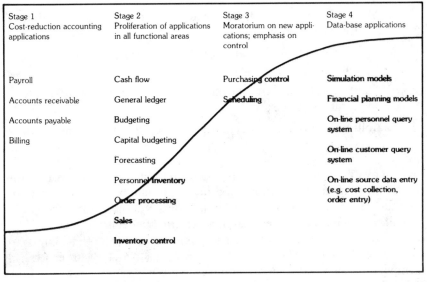

Stage 1 Cost-reduction accounting applications	Stage 2 Proliferation of applications in all functional areas	Stage 3 Moratorium on new applications; emphasis on control	Stage 4 Data-base applications
Payroll	Cash flow	Purchasing control	Simulation models
Accounts receivable	General ledger	Scheduling	Financial planning models
Accounts payable	Budgeting		On-line personnel query system
Billing	Capital budgeting		On-line customer query system
	Forecasting		On-line source data entry (e.g. cost collection, order entry)
	Personnel Inventory		
	Order processing		
	Sales		
	Inventory control		

INITIATION   CONTAGION   CONTROL   INTEGRATION

Reprinted by permission of *Harvard Business Review*. Exhibit from "Managing the Four Stages of EDP Growth," by Cyrus F. Gibson and Richard L. Nolan (January/February 1974). Copyright © 1974 by the President and Fellows of Harvard College; all rights reserved.

Management, May 1979) listed necessary qualities for the data manager. Among these requisites were:

1. A broad knowledge and ability to utilize the principles, concepts, methods, techniques, approaches, and systems of information management;

2. Ability to develop, apply, and adjust information plans and policies to attain objectives;

3. Ability to establish and maintain effective working relationships with all levels of management and with individual users and user groups;

4. Ability to apply sound, independent judgment in the solution of information problems;

5. Ability to compare actual information performance against information plans;

6. Ability to acquire a broad knowledge of the organization's total operating programs;

7. Ability to recycle existing information holdings to meet new project users.

Two innovative concepts emerge from Horton's checklist. One is that the firm's information and information problems should be at the forefront of the data manager's decisions. In order to understand the information problems of an organization, the data manager *must* understand the operation of that particular business. Such a statement sounds like nothing but common sense. Yet, in 1979, many data processing people were experts in manipulating data and using the computing machinery but knew very little about the actual operations of the businesses where they were employed.

A second and perhaps more important concept presented by Horton was the idea of the importance of involving the user in the actual search for pertinent data and the ability to work closely with the data processing people in the solution of information problems. Again, one would think that such involvement should be a "given." However, the history of data processing is littered with evidence of very little or no working relationships between those who utilize the data for business decisions and those who actually compile the data. As late as the summer of 1985, such a communications gap was discussed by Lawrence F. Young [208:70]. Young described a scenario in which a division manager for a large corporation was having difficulty finding a recent graduate to hire for a new information center support group. What the manager wanted was someone who "could com-

municate well with users, understand the problems, and help them solve their problems." The job required someone who was interested in the business itself and whose career path was not fused to a mainframe computer or a central DP department. Discussing the current (1985) trend for information specialists, Young stated: "The trend is toward MIS people with good business sense, who worry more about the bottom line than about the state of the computing art. This trend has manifested itself in many corporations by the elevation of MIS managers to the executive suite, where they are often known as chief information officers (CIO)" [208:70].

The Importance of User Involvement

In both of his last two stages, Richard Nolan mentioned the importance of the user and the need for more user involvement. In the 1980s, business became more and more aware of the need for user involvement. Microcomputers were principally responsible for increased user interest and also increased emphasis on user productivity. David King discussed user involvement by stating: "It is ludicrous for the DP staff to maintain that these same users are not aware of their own needs. The users may well need assistance to express their needs in data processing terms, but it is the responsibility of the *true* DP professional to educate users about the power of the computer." Difficulty in involving the user may not always be the fault of the data processing people. Because many users are afraid of the computer — afraid of showing that they do not understand computers, simply afraid of the unknown — these same users make it very difficult. Often, they cut off the communication lines at the end of their initial interview in which they list their information needs.

Proliferation of Microcomputers

Probably the one thing that gave rise to consciousness or awareness of the importance of the user was the entrance of the microcomputer. In a speech at the Society for Information Management meeting in Chicago in 1984, Dr. Richard Byrne stated:

> The personal computer has brought on a period of profound and genuine change in the worlds of people and business that has produced a breakthrough in the way we think about and use computers in our . . . business lives. . . . This breakthrough has occurred because of the enthusiasm of powerful nonusers — company executives — and their expectations of what personal computers can do to solve their business problems and make them more efficient managers. [37]

Microcomputers have proliferated during the 1980s, especially after the IBM PC was introduced. The November 1983 *EDP Analyzer* summarized the future effects of end-user computing by discussing a study performed by Xerox between 1970 and 1980. In 1970, according to this summary, end-user computing within Xerox was only a negligible part of the computer usage. By 1980, the end user consumed forty percent of the computer capacity. The study further predicted that by 1990, end-user computing will consume about seventy-five percent of it!

The use of micros in business was predicted to follow the same pattern given by Nolan for the use of the large mainframe computers. Byrne stated that "the growth will follow an S-shaped curve, and . . . many organizations are near the first knee of the curve. Once beyond that knee, usage will grow very rapidly indeed—to the point where it probably will overwhelm the information systems department" [37]. Communication between the user and the system developer has to be an ongoing effort in which the user becomes "emotionally" involved in the development. Otherwise, the users may receive a system that is not at all what they expected in terms of performance, accuracy, and quality.

Now that pertinent literature on the evolutionary changes in methods of recording and utilizing business information for management purposes has been presented, the next two chapters will present an analytical evaluation of these changes. Particular emphasis is given to the conceptual proposals for making information available to management.

3

Changing Concepts in Obtaining Management Information

Just as computer utilization has changed over time, so have ideas about how to obtain necessary management information. Chapter 2 traced the evolution of computer utilization in business, with emphasis on information handling.

This chapter presents an analytical evaluation of changing concepts toward techniques for obtaining information useful in management decision making. In this evaluation, particular attention is first given to reasons for the development of the "total systems" concept. How businesses became disenchanted with the "total systems" approach for acquiring management information is discussed next. Finally, the current status of the "total systems" idea, along with other pertinent present-day concepts in information systems development, is evaluated. Possible reasons for the current thinking in the MIS area are also presented.

Initial Computer Applications in Business

As the computer became accepted as a business tool, more and more firms felt the need to acquire one. At first, many businesses were happy just to have a computer in the organization and to be able to apply its use to such mundane operations as payroll and inventory. In fact, it was very popular for top management of this era to provoke laughter at industrial conventions by remarking that the only thing they knew about their company computers was that they were red. Generally, top management of this period was not expected to know anything about either the computer's applications or its potential. In fact, mere possession of a computer caused the company, and therefore, the management, to be considered a part of the "avant-garde."

Since computers were exceptionally fast, the most visible operations for this speed appeared to be those clerical applications that were highly labor-intensive. Consequently, the first computer applications for many firms were in the clerical area. Repetitive clerical operations such as payrolls, accounts receivables or payables, and inventory records were quickly computerized, often in a piecemeal fashion. Robert Head remarked that even if the first computers had been capable of handling sophisticated programs, the programmers and systems analysts of that period would not have been capable of utilizing their potential [87].

Initially, many companies bought computers as prestige factors, just to keep up with their competitors. Others actually visualized the computer's potential, but often purchased more computer power than they needed or were able to utilize. As with anything new and revolutionary, mistakes were certainly made during this period. However, in most computer installations, feelings of satisfaction and even elation usually resulted if the payroll program ran. People did not feel at ease with computers and were thankful for any application that could be implemented successfully.

Head related that "once a company had successfully computerized one or two of these basic applications it seemed logical to venture into other application areas" [87]. Experience in the use of the computer slowly evolved with more and more of the routine business operations being transferred to the computer. However, any drastic change in methods while daily operations continued necessarily involved a painful experience and often caused much organizational upheaval and discontent. To avoid these consequences, a majority of the first computer applications were simply the punched card methods transferred "as is" to the computer.

Reasons for Disenchantment with Computers

In several ways, such compromises led to disillusionment. One cause of disenchantment was the fear and trepidation which the changeover itself (even if it were gradual) elicited in the minds of the actual data processing people. Whenever they took a successful operation and made a conversion to computers, the possibility of failure always existed. In order to minimize this risk, very few changes were made when the firm's applications were transferred to computers.

Another feature which increased management's disenchantment was the reluctance of data processing people to tamper with programs after they were initially computerized. Furthermore, making the changes necessary for improvement called for a great deal of work, considerable cost, and much soul-searching. In a 1976 report to the Society for Management Information Systems, May Weber, a psychoanalyst, discussed the resistance to changes in established organizational procedures experienced by data processing personnel [196]. When confronted with the above-mentioned requirements, many firms and the management of those firms were eager, or at least willing, to postpone drastic changes.

As with most scarce resources, cost was another component. During the initial periods, exorbitantly high computer prices prevented any but the larger companies from purchasing a computer. Coupled with high cost was another factor influencing companies to refrain from such purchases. In describing this facet, Donald Sanders related that "it was generally agreed by most businessmen, including the top executives of computer manufacturing firms, that 8 or 10 of the big electronic "brains" would satisfy the demand for such devices. This must go down in history as one of the worst market forecasts of all time" [165].

Gradually, as was discussed in chapter 2, computers became an integral part of the business scene, with more and more applications being found for their speed. Though considerable progress was made in computerization of business information, much of the adaptation was accomplished in a haphazard manner. In discussing this era, Head stated that "applications were not designed to permit intercommunication among them, even though in the real life environment of company operations there was significant interaction among the parts of the organization whose activities had been computerized" [87].

As companies increased the number of computer applications, available computer storage became an additional problem. Most firms needing to purchase or rent auxiliary memory found costs for additional computer storage to be prohibitive. In the early 1960s, random access accounting machines capable of storing records for immediate access were used by some hospitals and business firms. However, the trade-off of having records immediately available versus the high cost again resulted in firms having to settle for the less exotic batch methods. Only in situations where immediate access to such records was essential to the mainstream operation of a business could cost be justified.

Another problem bottlenecking initial business utilization of computers was that very few management people had any training with computers. In fact, few in management even had a conception of the computer's potential. Some of the major universities, such as Texas A&M University, the University of Minnesota, and the University of Pennsylvania, did pioneer in offering both individual courses and degree programs in computer science. But the majority of colleges and universities in the early 1960s either could not afford a computer or did not have the experienced, qualified faculty for teaching such courses. Since many businesses felt that training their own employees was too costly, management in general remained ignorant of computer concepts.

A number of years later, many large companies realized the importance of overcoming this educational deficiency and established training courses especially for their management personnel. An example of one such course is that of the Southwestern Bell Telephone Company. This firm sent all their management of the middle level and above to a computer appreciation school where these managers actually wrote computer programs. But in the 1950s such training for management in general was just not available. Even ten years later, in the early 1960s, smaller companies still could not afford such training.

As more and more young people with computer knowledge entered business and as numerous executives were trained "in house," progress in computerization increased in many business firms. Yet a number of such organizations still confined their computer applications to such well-defined problems as the routine accounting functions.

Constantly emphasized in beginning computer appreciation courses and in numerous texts written for such courses is the fact that the computer is a high-speed moron. This characteristic of computers limits execution to well-defined problems. When the procedure is vague or where the problem itself is ill-structured, programming such applications is quite difficult. In instances where computer people did not communicate clearly what type of problems lend themselves to computer solutions, additional disenchantment among management personnel resulted. An article outlining the deadly sins of data processing people contained the comment "One thing that has done more to create credibility problems in the mind of users is a data processor's tendency to make incredibly optimistic estimates. This comes largely from our habit of overselling ourselves and our services. We simply must start telling it the way it is" [110].

At first, excitement over having a computer coupled with lack of knowledge about its potential caused many firms to utilize the computer in turning out stacks of paper. These were often so bulky and contained so much information that they were practically useless. The busy manager soon felt that he was drowning in a sea of paper, but receiving little information of value. Disillusionment with the computer in many instances stemmed from these reams of paper turned out at a very rapid rate and stacked on management's desks. In most instances, management people felt that they were not any better off with this additional information, and possibly that they were worse off. In contrast were those managers who resisted the idea of receiving exception reports. As Dr. Weber related in her 1976 report to the Society for Management Information Systems, "Managers know that only the exceptions are important, but they would 'rather see all the numbers,' a resistance which is a waste of time and paper if nothing more" [196].

For a while, the magic that seemed to be associated with computers was enough to insure that computers would be used in business operations. In addition, the first applications were for the heavily clerically-oriented operations. These applications were first since they almost instantly showed cost-reductions and since they were the easiest to adapt to programming. Managers initially, then, were happy with these tangible results and were assured that theirs was a progressive, innovative firm.

Growing Sophistication in Computer Utilization

In management itself and in applications designed for computer usage, the idea of exception reporting became popular. With the implementation of this concept, computers were programmed so that reports were written only when some particular figure was above or below an average or outside a tolerance level. When computers were finally utilized for exception reporting, only then did computer usage actually assist in management decision making. Prior to that time, no uniqueness distinguished the computer reports from the manual reports, unless it was the tremendous volume of the computer reports.

Development of "Total Systems"

Business operations in the United States became more complex as the 1950s progressed and as knowledge from World War II research became more generally available to management. During this period, the idea of applying the systems approach to management arrived. Along with this general systems idea, the concept of applying systems to various areas of management also appeared. Thus evolved the idea that all of the computer operations for a business could be woven into a "total" system. Integrating the entire amount of information needed for all business decisions was the basis of the "total systems" concept. This dream was at first advanced in the literature, and then became a very popular "buzz" word for the more progressive managers. On paper, the "total systems" idea appeared to be a remarkable one, a concept that would revolutionize management decision making. Conceptually, the thought of a "total system" seemed to be *the* solution to most of management's information problems.

Bringing this idea to fruition was very difficult, however. Many factors contributed to that difficulty. When the idea of using a system for managing information appeared, necessary computer hardware and software were not available. Hardware necessary to store the voluminous data needed for implementing such a system was very expensive, and software was not available. However, creative data processing people felt that it was only a matter of time and availability of money which kept the software from being created. Several of the more affluent firms reasoned that the investment in creating a "total" information system would certainly bring a profitable return. Therefore, many of these firms jumped on the "total systems" bandwagon.

Barriers to "Total Systems"

Even when large amounts of money were invested and when innovative data processing people were available to work on the system, these "total" information systems still eluded even the progressive firms. Among the many reasons for such failure, one of the largest was the behavioral aspect. Ideas which looked good on paper did not reflect the vital fact that people were essential in implementing these concepts. Peter G. W. Keen, in a 1976 address to the Society for Management Information Systems, discussed the fallacy in such thinking.

> Technicians in the computer field have concentrated on *design*, independent of *implementation*, assuming that the power of a good idea is enough to assure its adaptation.
> Reality is painfully different. "Good" ideas are not always accepted. Change is slow and invariably incremental, requiring nuture and constant facilitation. It cannot simply be mandated. The introduction of any technical innovation into an organization brings uncertainty — even threat — and makes effective, established routines obsolete. [105]

The behavioral implications of such drastic changes to organizational status, power structures, employee relationships, informal and formal channels of communication, etc., were not considered in the plans for devising the "total" information system.

Chief among the behavioral problems associated with "total systems" was the resistance to change that was prevalent wherever such an idea was proposed. Organizational behavior follows human behavior in general, and the natural reaction is to resist anything new, different, or threatening to the status quo. The entire gamut of changes in organizational status, procedure, and structure resulting from computers themselves was greatly resisted. When people envisioned the potential upheaval which could result from the "total system" concept, resistance was even stronger.

According to Weber, the dominating force instigating such resistance was "fear — fear of total inadequacy, of annihilation" [196]. Weber also explained that she felt such resistance was "produced by the same intelligence and competence that produced the need for such services in the first place." Discussing the analogy between resistance to MIS and resistance to psychoanalysis, Weber further remarked that once the resistance is understood and overcome, "the energies previously given over to a restrictive measure are reinvested profitably and expansively." However, such insights were not predominant when the first "total" systems were proposed. Originally, the total system concept focused heavily on proper design at the expense of human considerations.

Furthermore, the concept of collecting all the needed information for management entailed a tremendous volume of data, which had never before been integrated. The sheer size of the task itself was overwhelming. Building information systems took time. The complete information necessary to run a modern-day business could not be totally integrated in a day, week, month, or even a year.

The broad planners failed to consider the day-to-day implications of such implementations. As attempts were made to devise a "total" information system, these pitfalls became apparent. The beautiful idea which appeared to be the answer to a crucial business problem now seemed to be "an ugly duckling." As firms poured more and more money into data processing and received fewer and fewer visible accomplishments for the dollars spent, further disillusionment set in. Company presidents became leery of the data processing people who asked for larger and larger budgets when the output of these departments appeared to be little better than last year's efforts. Information necessary for any decision above the first-line operational management level just did not seem to be available regardless of how much time, effort, and money was invested.

Little by little, the "total systems" concept fell into disrepute. People who espoused such an idea soon were classified as "dreamers." Yet, there still was a desperate need for information which could assist management personnel above the operational level. Some dreamers just do not give up in spite of setbacks; such were many of the people in the data processing field. Instead of attempting to computerize the entire volume of business information, a few of these dedicated people conceived the idea of integrating a firm's information gradually through "modules," or subsystems. Thus, the creators began with two or three areas of business which were closely interrelated and consolidated the information from these sources. Payroll and personnel information, inventory and accounts payable, budget and production operations are all examples of such areas which lend themselves to integration. These consolidated systems did produce results that were visible, although many times such programs could not be given a dollars-and-cents evaluation. Improved customer relations, better employee morale, fewer shortages, and such results are difficult to assess in dollar terms, yet it is evident that they all contribute to more efficient business operation.

In discussing the subsystem approach, Head stated that "the resultant system was uneven in quality, reflecting the proficiency of the technical personnel assigned at one time." He further commented that there was "an unevenness in their quality, ranging from excellent to very marginal in design concept and operational performance" [87]. Characteristics of this period were the inexperience of the systems analysts, the increasing data processing budgets, and the lack of visible, tangible results. Such problems for data processing people prompted *Time* magazine to write an article on computer utilization and to remark that "the honeymoon is over." Top management suddenly became aware of "runaway" computer budgets, and frequently concluded that the only way to control them was through drastic measures [35].

In an article discussing the "Four Stages of EDP Growth," Cyrus Gibson and Richard Nolan remarked that "action taken to deal with such a crisis often goes beyond what is needed and the pendulum may swing too far. . . . All this can occur at the expense of full resource utilization in the long run" [73]. Either these extreme reactions of management caused computer personnel to leave the company or these people were more cautious about introducing innovative applications. Either result was to the detriment of the information needs of the organization. The effect was that applications that had real potential for increasing revenues and profit were left untouched. Introduction of strong controls often either stymied growth or stopped it altogether.

An epitomization of this period was given by Fred Gruenberger.

> The computer in business, especially in management information systems, has been the butt of inside humor — much of it snide — and this, like the jokes about the Pennsylvania Railroad, was probably the forerunner of a period of disenchantment which is now beginning to show itself in some business managements' reappraisals of *where* their management information systems have *taken* them. Not only *where* have they been *taken*, but for how much! [80]

Current Status of Management Information Systems

With increased acceptance of computers, manufacturers began to improve their hardware. Manufacturing in volume brought about lower costs for both computer memory and peripheral equipment. In addition, improved and innovative technology also lowered prices of computer components. Furthermore, increased experience with writing computer software also expedited the creation of better methods for storing and retrieving information. Such improvements and innovations again made many of the features of the "total systems" concept appear feasible. Summarizing the situation in a 1965 report, E. G. Canning wrote with optimism that both hardware and software developments were progressing, but that applications knowledge was lagging. He further stated that "under these conditions, it would not be valid to say that Management Information Systems are still in the 'visionary stage' " [39].

As computer prices decreased and improved software became available, the prospect for better management information systems also improved. Once more, the larger, more affluent, more progressive companies began to toy with the idea of the "total" system. But, having once been burned, they were very cautious. Instead of quickly attempting to implement such systems, they now were willing to spend necessary time in studying the feasibility of computer applications. While spending time and money for feasibility studies, they were also willing to investigate the possibility of devising better operational methods. Furthermore, business management was now aware of the importance of the human aspect in any successful business undertaking. Firms were now conditioned to realize the necessity of considering behavioral factors.

Among the behavioral factors to be considered were human fears of the computer, organizational upheaval caused by changes in information acquisition, and implications involved in any shift in the organizational power structure or employee relations. In his book, *Why Information Systems Fail*, Henry Lucas discussed the importance of considering the myriad facets of human interaction.

> The success of an information system is highly dependent upon the relationship between users and the information services department and on the use of the system. Concentration on the technical aspect of systems and a tendency to overlook organizational behavior problems and users are reasons most information systems have failed. [124]

In a talk before the Society for Management Information Systems in 1975, Herbert Halbrecht echoed these thoughts by stating that the manager of MIS is not only managing technology but also managing change. Halbrecht further commented that "the role as a change agent is an extraordinarily sensitive one and therefore, it is threatening to other people" [82].

Since 1969, millions of dollars have been spent on developing management information systems, with few successful results before 1975. A number of articles discussed the problems of this period and features complicating these problems. Particularly enlightening was a 1974 article by Robert Waggener, in which the author proposed measures for "restoring systems' tarnished charisma," and then related how the glamour and mysticism of data processing were being replaced by disillusionment [193]. In a similar article, James R. Johnson reported that companies must still work toward a viable information system even though the obstacles seem formidable. His argument was that "progress in this area of computer usage has been judged essential to an organization's existence. Those companies not profiting from the huge potential payoff may simply not stay competitive" [100]. This theme was still echoed in 1985, with articles and books calling the computer a "competitive advantage" and depicting the success of one firm after another as dependent on management's ability to use the information system to get ahead of the competition.

Companies in 1975 still aspired for a "total" information system, but realized such a system must be developed gradually. Furthermore, firms were then aware of many of the painful lessons of the past and of the steps necessary to avoid previous mistakes. The potential for having needed information available for decision making was well worth the effort. Therefore, the search for an integrated information system was not abandoned.

In this search for integrated systems, the classic approach was called the "bottom-up" approach. Beginning with a simple function such as the payroll, the designer then added another function until the major functions were combined into one system. Paul Gross and Robert Smith described such an approach by stating that "major functional areas (payroll, inventory control, costing) are considered as separate subsystems under the control of a master program which monitors subsystem integration" [79]. In the early 1970s, the opposite approach gained acceptance; this approach is called "top-down." In essence, such an approach considers the overall picture and then fills in the parts to make up the whole. Since the "top-down" approach to integrated systems was not available for most of the time period of the original literature search, no distinction was made in the original survey. However, for the 1985 survey, "top-down" methodology was very prevalent and in wide use by many firms.

At the conclusion of the 1975 research, few companies had really perfected the idea of an information system which could assist operational, tactical, and strategical levels of management in decision making. In the interim since 1975, many breakthroughs have been made in these areas. Management has increasingly recognized the computer as a tool which can indeed make them more productive. Conditions seem much more promising for successful management information systems with increased computer awareness, the introduction of micros, the decline in prices, and the advances in both storage and software. Chapter 4 details current happenings in these areas and also presents many of the changing concepts for the management information systems field.

4

Current Concepts in Obtaining Management Information

The common questions asked in the 1980s about information systems and methods of obtaining management information are:

1. Are there common characteristics for successful information systems?

2. Have developers changed their ideas about the important steps in developing such systems?

3. What has caused differences in the 1980s in the development of information systems?

4. Are there fundamental concepts that are so classic that they have remained even as technology has advanced?

Before attempting to answer these questions in a straightforward manner, one needs a background in information concepts being currently implemented. A background in application developments would also be helpful. Concepts discussed in this chapter that help to answer the above questions are: structured analysis, design, and programming; decision support systems; prototyping; fourth-generation languages; information centers; program and application generators; and workbenches.

Recent applications of computers for obtaining information involved on-line, real-time systems along with the use of terminals and complicated networks. Paul Gross and Robert Smith describe these recent applications and compare them to the past, stating that "in the middle to late 1960s theoretically computer developments permitted instantaneous managerial decision at all levels of management. . . . In reality, few organizations developed such levels of sophisticated decision making." They further relate that the real obstacle preventing such development is the problem of developing data bases [79:55]. Currently, in the mid-1980s, firms that desire a viable information system are installing data bases. Many firms have been quite successful with their data bases, and many companies have grown just by supplying the software for data base installations.

Along with data bases, many other practices have gained both managerial approval and acceptance because these practices have made information available on a more timely basis. These practices will be listed and then presented in a more detailed manner in later paragraphs. Structured design and structured programming are two of these concepts that have been accepted almost universally wherever data processing has been successful. Just recently, attempts to improve and shorten the development of successful information systems have brought about fourth-generation computer languages, prototyping, program and application generators, information centers, decision support systems, and workbenches. According to David King [109:8], the 1970s saw structured techniques of software development emerge as the best solution for making software development predictable and manageable. However, the newly emerging software tools of the 1980s made prototyping using fourth-generation languages tremendously more productive than using structured methodologies with COBOL (under certain conditions).

Structured Methods of Analysis and Design

In his introductory chapter, David King discusses the systems development life cycle (SDLC) by stating that it "offers a way for DP and user management to monitor, control, and understand what is going on." [109:1]. Developing systems that would assist in solving management's need for information appeared to be tremendously difficult for the first data processing people. Because a large data processing system consisted of so many complex tasks and dependencies, the concept of dividing the development process into a series of smaller, simpler tasks was initiated. The standard method for developing a large system assumed a series of sequential steps, with each step producing documentation and a "deliverable" before the next step was undertaken. Because this method gave management needed control and enabled them to make reasonably accurate and consistent estimates of development time, the use of the SDLC was "growing rapidly even exponentially as the successful experiences with SDLCs increase" [109:6].

The ability of this system development method to deal with large, complex systems in an orderly, systematic fashion was another of its advantages. "By applying the divide-and-conquer strategy, we realize that this enormous activity was manageable" [109:8].

Systems Development Life Cycle

David Katch, in the foreword to David King's book, writes:

> Over the past fifteen years, the field of software application development has progressed
> very slowly, but steadily from an art form to a semi-disciplined approach. This approach
> embraces the notion that one can build consistently better systems using a phased system
> life cycle for development. [109:xii]

When the research for the original Delphi questions concerning systems
development life cycle was conducted in 1974–76, no such consensus of
opinion about developing viable information systems existed. Over the
eight- to ten-year period since the author's original research, a body of
knowledge has evolved to the point that almost any book discussing the
development of information systems lists stages of development. Granted,
these stages may vary from as many as twelve to as few as four, but all of
them present the idea that a systematic, disciplined approach should be used
in developing information systems. "Systems development life cycle"
(SDLC) is the term that has gained wide acceptance. Where no such agreement or method existed ten to fifteen years ago, today the concept of a
development cycle is invariably a "given."

Structured Programming

Applying similar structuring to the programs that make up the information
system was a subset of the systems development life cycle. The program
designer looked at the overall whole and then divided it into smaller and
smaller segments. An overall "driver" program was written, with subrou-
tines covering the separate parts. The program can then be given to more
than one programmer. However, each person writing a part of the whole
must apply rules, format procedures, naming rules, and standards for producing codes that logically fit into the driver program.

Structuring computer programs yielded many benefits and overcame
many of the problems inherent in previous programming methods. Consistent formatting rules and naming standards made it possible for other programmers to understand and possibly maintain such programs. When a
standard pattern for program construction was followed, quite often only
the more difficult part of the program needed to be created. Other standard
parts, such as input/output portions, could be reused—thus eliminating
costly debugging time. Control of programming time and costs was much
less difficult where structured programming was followed. Also, with this
method beginning programmers could be given parts of a complex program
where they would not be asked to work on a large program initially.

As with structured design and the SDLC, structured programming has been widely accepted in both academic and industrial circles. With widespread utilization, improvements, and innovations, the application of structured ideas is gaining favor. Furthermore, companies are noting more and more advantages of these methods.

Summarizing the past applications and glancing into the future, David King remarks:

> The near and midterm future of DP applications programming certainly belongs to the modern, structured languages. . . . the growth in DP applications over the last three decades will seem like a snail's pace compared with the meteoric growth that has just started . . . . If (these new tools) . . . are applied in a coordinated and integrated fashion throughout the systems development life cycle, . . . [they] could revolutionize the way that systems are being developed and implemented. [109:15]

Fourth-Generation Languages

Since the advent of the computer, manufacturers have constantly tried to find a way to make the use of computers easier. Previously, computer languages progressed from the actual "bits and bytes" of machine language through assemblers toward "higher-level languages." Even such well-known higher-level languages as COBOL, FORTRAN, PL/1, ALGOL, and BASIC are still not that "easy" to use. The invention of the personal computer increased the desire in more and more people to use these machines in obtaining needed information quickly. Creative people thus came up with what is known as "fourth-generation languages" to meet this need.

Many writers made the distinction between "procedural" languages such as COBOL, where specific syntax must be followed, and "nonprocedural" languages, which were thought to be English-like. The *EDP Analyzer* recognized this trend by publishing a small special report entitled "Fourth Generation Languages and Prototyping" [70]. In this book, the characteristics of such a language were listed as non-procedural, more natural, and allowing human language-type of dialogue between the programmer and the computer.

Discussing the fourth-generation language concept, David King remarks

> As the procedural languages become easier to use, simultaneously the non-procedural, user-friendly languages will begin to take over. Today's high-level, structured languages will appear restrictive and clumsy compared with the human-language oriented, conversational program development techniques of the future. Structured programming will eventually prove to have been only a phase, albeit a very important phase, in the movement of DP program development from an esoteric black art to an efficient, ubiquitous "business process." [109:15]

One important difference in a fourth-generation language is that there are commands which perform a complete function. Simple terms, often one word, can be used instead of having to detail the steps which the computer program must follow. Examples of such commands are SORT (file Z on field X) and SELECT (all records with a value in a particular field). With a minimum amount of time, effort, and retention of the language details, most users obtain needed information using a fourth-generation language.

Discussing ways in which fourth-generation languages can be used to create new programs, Roger Sisson lists: producing analytic ad hoc reports from a data base; creation of prototypes of complex systems by DP professionals; and creation of simple applications by end users. [175:9]. For the ad hoc reports, Sisson claims that the user receives the report forty times faster than if he requests the report from a programmer and has to wait for the results to be programmed in a procedural language. He also claims that the DP pros can write complete, complex application systems in one-fifth to one-tenth the time as compared to using procedural languages.

Many fourth-generation languages (4GL) are especially useful for ad hoc queries since they permit users to key in commands to retrieve information from files or a data base. In addition, many of these languages can guide users by prompting them with menus or dialogues. According to the *EDP Analyzer* report, "Users can create new files with the 4GL and can maintain existing files that use 4GL-acceptable formats . . . . The 4GL should provide the important supplementary functions for file maintenance as well as transaction validation, logging, and so on" [70:11].

Mary Rich, an independent consultant in El Segundo, California [70:12–14], has been using fourth-generation languages over a period of seven years to help replace old business applications. The languages she has used are RAMIS and RAMIS II from Mathematica Corporation of Princeton, New Jersey. Her experience has been that replacing COBOL programs with interactive RAMIS II systems has resulted in programs that tend to have fewer errors in them than the systems they replace because the RAMIS II programs are simpler. Remarkable is her statement that a 100–line RAMIS II program has replaced a 6000–line COBOL program and led to a more accurate system. According to her report "users are happier with the system, and it continues to grow" [70:14].

As a caution to prospective users, Rich recommends that 4GLs not be used for applications requiring real-time updating, multiple terminal updating, or very high volume. In addition, she recommends that before the programmers begin coding they spend time doing systems analysis work. This caution highlighted how an inexperienced programmer could run into trouble if he or she did not spend time thinking through the problem before beginning coding.

F. J. Grant has recently written on the disadvantages of using fourth-generation languages. According to Grant, these languages are not the panacea that everyone has sought; that is, not every situation in information processing lends itself to fourth-generation languages. Grant asks: "For example, if a 4GL product saves 50% of the time needed to code . . . but requires 50% to 150% more CPU and disk resources, is this an increase in productivity?" [78:99]. The remainder of Grant's discussion centers on the need to emphasize and work with structuring data. He states that "much progress remains to be made in understanding and managing corporate data resources." Remarking that the biggest problem is not with the languages used as much as it is with the data itself, Grant concludes by stating, "In general, the information sent back up the chain of command is not complete, does not meet the requirement, or results in another request for information to be broken out in a different way" [78:100].

Prototyping

Closely connected to the use of fourth-generation languages is the idea of prototyping. In a paper on software prototyping, Jenkins and Naumann present the idea that a data processing prototype is a first attempt at a design which is generally extended and enhanced [70:40]. David King defines a prototype as "an original version or model on which a completed software system is formed . . . a prototype is developed as an early, unrefined version of the system so that users and developers alike can gain experience with the system" [109:184].

Currently, the prototype approach has been used by several accounting and consulting firms in the systems development approach. Using a prototype calls for close management involvement, allows them to see results quickly, and then allows for changes without accompanying costs and delays. On the negative side, prototypes rapidly constructed on a micro add to the difficulty of convincing management that developing a similar system for a mainframe must take considerably more time.

Franz Edelman of RCA, a pioneer in the use of software prototyping, describes the process as a "quick and inexpensive process of developing and testing a trial balloon" [70:8]. A big advantage is that the prototype is a live, working system, not just an idea on paper. Because the system is visible and performing actual work, both the designer and prospective end-user can evaluate the potentiality of the proposed system.

For traditional procedural language programs, changes have always been costly and time-consuming. However, prototypes created with fourth-generation languages are relatively inexpensive to build and are created quickly. Speed and lower cost, along with the ability to make changes rapidly, are all reasons for the wide acceptance of prototypes. Past system development life cycles have been quite lengthy, but today's executive cannot afford to wait for two years to solve a problem concerning information needed this week. Thus the idea of prototyping has been embraced by both the designer and the user as an excellent solution whose time has come.

Decision Support Systems

Information used by executives in solving crucial, immediate problems has given rise to the term "decision support system" (DSS). Along with the idea of having a pool of company facts and figures in a data base came the idea of tapping into that reservoir on an ad hoc basis. Rather than having the periodic reports from the DP community, as had been the order of the day in most DP operations, executives feel that creation of company data bases should make more timely information available to them. In fact, from the first computer purchase, many advocates feel that such immediate data access should be soon forthcoming. As most studies of historical computer development will reveal, many factors have led to disenchantment and the realization that data for decision making was difficult to have available on an instant's notice.

After numerous companies struggled with the creation of data bases and made these available on-line, decision support systems seemed much more viable and possible. In fact, as computer facilities improved, terminals accessing these data bases have become a reality in many organizations. Query languages have been developed to make inquiries about one-time problem solutions feasible, and the idea of decision support systems has come out of the academic realm and into the "real world."

According to Richard M. Denise, "The first DSS alternative most managers become aware of is the personal computer." Mr. Denise then states that VISICALC and other spreadsheet programs have become the status symbols and "the ultimate executive enhancement tool of the 80s" [61:207]. His article was written before the introduction of VISICALC's replacement, Lotus 1-2-3, so that this concept could be even more emphasized today. Spreadsheet use in the analysis of problems and in the conversion of many of these problems to graphic presentations has further enhanced the concept of decision support systems.

The "ideal" decision support system is a comprehensive software system encompassing everything a manager needs: highly flexible, adaptable data base management; powerful modeling capabilities; a wide range of easily accessible statistical and mathematical techniques; presentation-quality graphics; and report writing. All of these should be available in one user-friendly, interactive DSS available through a desktop terminal. Such a listing sounds like an impossible dream because this system is truly an ideal, quite costly, and probably unavailable in many organizations. Yet, establishment of such a comprehensive software system would certainly go a long way in assisting most managers in the decision-making process.

Listing some of the shortcomings of DSS with a microcomputer, Denise states that in many instances "personal computers are limited to take advantage of the corporate-wide database" [61:209]. Downloading parts of the data base has been possible in many DP operations. Often, then, a portion of the data base may supply all the information needed by managers in their search for decision-assisting information. One of the primary limiting factors delaying or at least slowing down decision support activities has been the sizeable investment in hardware, software, and people that a true decision support system entails. Depending on the company's priorities, a host of attractive alternatives has been available to supply top management with one or more of the broad range of capabilities generally known as "decision support."

The encouraging thought here is that the cost of decision support systems is coming down as more and more programs are adaptable to micros, as the cost of microsoftware declines, and as less expensive ways are discovered to tap the mainframe data bases. Innovations in decision support are constantly being introduced. Among some of the most current are the graphic packages, the "window" effect that enables one to look at several parts of a program at once, and the executive scheduler.

As with all other areas of computing and its application to business problems, the communication between user and computer people is of vital importance. As Denise states, "It is the glue holding the integrated DSS together" [61:211]. Therefore, the data processing people must understand management's true needs and understand the organization for which they are working. On the other hand, executives from the top down must be "committed to making the investment in money, manpower, and time spent learning to take advantage of a system capable of revolutionizing the way they work and think" [61:5].

Information Centers

Most articles describing the current (1985) state of computing in business at least mention the applications backlog that exists in many data processing departments. In order to circumvent lengthy delays, users are becoming more sophisticated in using computers. Increased literacy has been especially boosted by the proliferation of micros. Fourth-generation languages coupled with decision support systems have also given impetus to the use of micros.

As end users have expressed the desire to utilize micros and fourth-generation languages to create their own application programs, companies have recognized the advantage of "user-driven" computing. To assist these users information centers (ICs) have been developed in many companies. To adequately maintain and control user-driven computing, development of an information center has become almost essential. These centers assist the user in whatever way is necessary—from teaching them fourth-generation languages to technical support in developing mainframe connections. Another purpose of the information center is to provide data availability as requested and as meets the company guidelines for accessibility.

Ad hoc consulting, providing the end user with advice when situations arise that the end user is unable to handle, is also one of the tasks many information centers perform. The center may be in charge of developing some means of effective downloading of selected data from the mainframe system in a form usable by electronic spreadsheets. Discussing the problems of information centers, Shirley Eis remarks that one of the chief concerns today is the proliferation of products on the market. A manager needing information quickly does not have much time to devote to the learning process. Therefore, she notes, "nontechnical people still found themselves with an unsatisfactorily high level of complexity. Software tools use incompatible languages and data structures and data linkage is virtually nonexistent" [66:41].

Expounding on this problem, Eis explains that each of the so-called nonprocedural languages has from twenty to fifty separate commands which a manager needs to master for minimal literacy. With different products for report generators, graphic prompters, and modeling tools, the manager is then called upon to face an almost impossible time constraint. She remarks that "more corporations are beginning to look for a way to bring coherence to their ICs" [66:41]. A condensation of her discussion shows that the requisites are threefold:

1. IC staff must be free to choose the best product for their environment;

2. Roadblocks to users must be removed (i.e., users should be taught enough about the product to satisfy their immediate needs, and then more as they request it);

3. Users must have automatic access to the relevant data bases regardless of which product controls the data (i.e., there must be a data base management system capable of interacting with all of the products used).

James Martin, writing in *The Information Manifesto,* makes two very strong statements concerning information centers. First, he writes "the growth of information centers is the most vigorous new trend in DP management." He also states that "the information center is the management vehicle for end-user computing." Listing a number of reasons why a company should have such a system, Martin particularly emphasizes the importance of the end user.

Naturally, a combination of Martin's list and that of Eis would give an ideal information center. Although few companies will reach that plateau, eight percent of the Fortune 1000 companies have achieved near total integration on both software product levels and a data level. Such an achievement has shielded the users from having to tackle the computer system's inherent complexity. Eis also explained that another thirty-five percent of ICs have made some advancement in the ease of use of individual products. As she succinctly explains: "Simplicity is being achieved not by eliminating complexity, but by hiding that complexity behind sophisticated software" [66:41].

Especially valuable to the entire organization is the simplification of applications programs made by teaching users new techniques. Facilities suitable for end users include simple or complex query languages, report generators, application generators, graphics languages, and the very high level fourth-generation languages available within the company.

The most important task for the information center is training, with members of the center being able to specialize in parts of the technology. These specialists should then be able to communicate their knowledge to the end user. Communication with the end user is again of vital concern because users of the information center are the ultimate customers. Information specialists must be familiar with and able to talk in the language of the end user. In a similar situation, the emphasis should be upon meeting the user's real needs. The establishment of the information center has been identified as the best way to reduce backlogs and improve user relationships. Just as the original higher-level computer languages were invented to make programming a computer easier for the masses, so the idea of integrating complex software has brought the user into the decision support systems of the present.

Application and Program Generators

Several other tools have been developed to speed up the systems development life cycle and improve the productivity of programmers. Classed together are two of these: program and application generators. Both of these are pieces of software designed to take much of the drudgery from program coding itself. Instead of writing a program from scratch, one can be assisted in the program writing by a software package called a program generator. These packages can be used to generate or produce applications, programs, code, reports, etc.

What is the difference between an application generator and a program generator? According to Canning,

> An application generator accepts input data (the parameters for the application) and generates computer code for performing the complete application. A program generator, on the other hand, generates code for one program at a time. To create a complete system using a program generator, a number of programs generally have to be specified and created. [70:9]

One can easily see how the idea of these two generators fits into the desire to speed up the systems development of a business project. In reducing the time spent on such a process, a generator of either type should be easy to use and flexible. Typically, the user inputs to a generator many of the same items input to a fourth-generation language: data definitions, output report specifications, and formats. Because the ultimate goal is often ease of use, many of these generators use a menu or question-and-answer session, and some allow this input to be entered on-line.

From the information given, the application generator creates a complete computer code (possibly COBOL) which must be compiled before it can be run. On the other hand, the program generator may produce source code which can be modified directly without using the generator. As with all the newer methods, structured methodologies and standards for coding and data names are required.

The tremendous cost of developing computer applications along with the time necessary for such development caused companies to search for generators or productivity tools to cut down on both cost and time. Jan Snyders presents the idea that "Generators Do the Trick" [179:212]. The major benefit Snyders lists is increased productivity. She gives several examples, one of which is the Seattle (Washington) Housing Authority. The authority director, using UFO, an OXFORD software package, experienced about a tenfold increase in productivity as compared to programming in COBOL.

In the same article, Snyders reports on the short training period required to use the application generator. She states that five days is the total time required to master the entire system, but that in a matter of four hours almost anyone can become productive with the system. In order to document the ease of maintenance, Snyders interviews David Farrell, a Harvard University systems planner. Rather than buying a package for the accounting system and then modifying the package, Harvard bought an application generator, *Generation Five*. Farrell explains that by using this generator he has been able to improve their accounting system significantly. A decided advantage of this particular generator is its flexibility.

Snyders also gives a sampling of application generators under several classifications. Among the generators listed under "Report Writers" were Cullinane's CULPRIT, Data Management's DATASCAN, Enterprise Technology's GRS, Informatic's INQUIRY IV, ANSWER/2, ANSWER/DB, Information Builder's FOCUS, Intel's REPORT WRITER, and Intel's GENIUS [179:210–26].

Workbenches

All of the tools mentioned above are useful in increasing productivity in the design of information systems and in the management access to valuable information. Each technology, however, requires a certain amount of learning time and some encouragement for the user, especially the non-programming end user. An answer to the phenomenon of shortening the time period and making productivity tools easier to use is the "workbench."

Various types of workbenches have been developed and several definitions apply to this concept. The principal idea is to combine a variety of available, useful programming and design tools into a usable whole, making these available and easy to use. The *EDP Analyzer* for April 1985 discusses three application development workbench tools. One of these is a packaged approach called DESIGN/1, developed and provided by one of the Big Eight U.S. accounting firms, Arthur Andersen and Company. Their project team workbench provides automated documentation facilities for text, graphics, and data. A standardized format may be used for the documentation or it may be free-form. As an integral part of the workbench, DESIGN/1 also has (1) a system dictionary for holding field name definitions, (2) data design and screen design facilities, (3) a prototyping facility for demonstrating the flow of a program, and (4) publishing facilities for printing documents, such as screens, report, structure charts, etc. ("Speeding Applications Development," p.14)

Many of these workbenches have a programmer's workbench where the repetitious modules, such as reports and inputs, can be prewritten in skeletal form and made available to the programmer. An increasing number of companies are using these technological advances to increase the productivity of their programmers. The key to the whole idea is to make these complex methods transparent to the user; as with the software for the use of fourth-generation languages, experienced programmers can bring all these tools together for easy access. Instead of having to use the tools separately and having to search for a way to combine their usefulness, companies that have developed workbenches have combined these tools into a useful package. The user, then, is not lost in the maze of pieces of software, but can switch from graphics to text to data — all on the same system.

The challenge facing most organizations is how to integrate these new tools to achieve massive productivity gains. Some consultants have said that with a fourth-generation language, it is no longer necessary to think about structured techniques. Others contend that structured development may need improvement in the area of user friendliness, but that it is even more important in a fourth-generation environment because:

1. It is much easier to develop complicated systems with a 4GL and structured techniques are necessary to guide the breaking of larger problems into manageable smaller pieces;

2. Structured techniques allow clear communication and will speed the development of new systems;

3. Using 4GLs will also shorten the cycle and improve the enhancement and maintenance process during production. [70]

The most difficult process is to blend both structured techniques and 4GLs to achieve optimum performance. An interaction between these two essential 1980s technologies is essential for successful system design and implementation.

Now that the information concepts currently being implemented have been presented and a cursory look has been taken at applications developments, the questions asked at the beginning of the chapter should be approached.

There are many common characteristics for successful information systems. These characteristics can be culled from just the discussions in this chapter; namely, such systems present timely information in a form that the user can both understand and use. Furthermore, such a presentation must be relatively easy to acquire and cost-effective.

Developers have changed their ideas about developing systems, but have not deserted the systems development life cycle. Although such things as prototypes, 4GLs, generators, and information centers may shorten the actual development time, intense analysis is still necessary if the programs developed are to meet the user's needs. What has actually occurred, as outlined in the *EDP Analyzer* for April 1985, is that users have been willing to accept the newer tools while retaining the systematic control invoked by the systems development life cycle method.

Two primary causes of differences in developing information systems in the 1980s are evident: the advent of the microcomputer and the tremendous decline in the cost of both computer hardware and software. The fact that information today is being used as a competitive weapon might also be added to this list. At any rate, the micro revolutionized information demands within even the smaller firms. Prior to the microcomputer's appearance, managers had a desire for information of all types, but knew that the cost of obtaining such information would be prohibitive. Not so today. With the added fact that many new productivity tools are being developed, one can see a great deal of difference — but it all can be traced back to the micro and cost.

Fundamental concepts dealing with information management have been developed over the past twenty years. These have become classic and have remained even as technology has advanced. Paramount among these is the idea that information is the "life blood" of a business; it is just as valuable as the four M's of production (men, money, material, and machines), and it *can* be managed. As advanced technology has made much of the organization's information more readily accessible, more and more emphasis has been given to the importance of information. Forward-looking companies are currently seeking ways in which computer technology and data availability can be used as a competitive advantage.

5

Critical Factors in the Phases
of Conceptual Design

The research in the first edition of this book gave particular attention to eight phases applicable to the conceptual design of a management information system. These phases were: (1) Feasibility study, (2) Requirements analysis, (3) System specifications, (4) System design, (5) Coding and programming, (6) Testing, (7) Documentation, and, (8) Implementation.

As each of these phases is analyzed in this chapter, a definition is presented. The critical factors for each phase are then discussed in the light of the opinions of recognized writers in the information systems field. From a composite of the thinking of these well-known authorities, a set of criteria for developing each phase has been assembled.

Phase One: Feasibility Study

Various definitions have been proposed for the term "feasibility study," but the following definition has been used in this book: A feasibility study is one which looks at the possibility of integrating present ways of obtaining business information and combining these methods into a system. In this context, "possibility" includes both economic as well as technological concepts.

Many factors have been interwoven in the concept of feasibility, as evidenced from this quote from *Business Systems*, a 1970 book published by the Association of Systems Management.

> During the mushrooming growth of the data processing field, the title of "feasibility study" has been applied to studies of widely varying scope. They vary in nature from a cursory overall survey of what can be done with automated equipment to an extensive and intensive program of survey, design and implementation. We hoped to establish somewhat a middle-of-the-road definition in this chapter. . . . we will recognize as a feasibility study any broadscope survey involving data processing. . . . [this] implies a study of the practicability of a proposed action. [13]

Various authors consulted have presented definitions which are similar. A study of categories which these writers have discussed under the term "feasibility study" revealed that a whole gamut of ideas had been considered. Included were very narrow definitions which discussed only whether or not a computer should be installed. Others were very broad coverages defining a variety of activities. In this latter group, the range of activities included part or all of the steps necessary for diagnosing the problems of a business, studying all the relationships and interrelations of the business, and considering various alternative solutions with their advantages and disadvantages.

Classifying the steps in analysis and design of a management information system was quite arbitrary. Wide varieties of methods were employed by the many authors consulted. Ideas concerning ways to effectively design a system were similar in many instances, but approaches for presenting these ideas varied extensively.

Depending on the organization and presentation of the material, numerous authors made no mention of some of the selected facets chosen for this paper and outlined at the start of this chapter. Certain of these phases were not pertinent to a particular author's selected method of presentation for some of the books consulted. However, in most of the writings all of the categories were at least mentioned somewhere, even if they were not discussed in detail.

In a majority of the writings, these different phases in the conceptual design of a management information system were so inextricably intertwined that one would have difficulty determining where one phase ended and the next phase began. Semantic differences were also quite prevalent, with one writer using the same phrases in discussing "feasibility study" that another author employed in defining "requirements analysis." Because of the chosen arrangements of information by individual writers, ideas they presented did not always fall under the specific headings selected for this research. However, if these ideas were discussed by particular authors under any category or label, the thoughts were included in the tabulations.

Indicative of the arbitrariness of segregating or partitioning of MIS conceptual design is the quote from Leonard Krauss:

> The human side of MIS can no more be neatly confined to some arbitrarily defined part of the system than we can confine its considerations to this particular section of the book. It permeates almost everything in MIS. Some of the human factors are rather pedestrian, and some are related to the advent of MIS, although this in itself does not make them new. [114:127]

Evidences of the different approaches may be viewed in a comparison of the presentation of John Burch and Felix Strater [33:243] and that of David H. Li [119:5-6]. Burch and Strater proposed the idea that the feasibility aspects require that "one continually ask whether or not something is feasible." Then, these authors reiterated the same idea by stating that a "feasibility analysis helps determine the likelihood that the recommendations proposed . . . can be carried out." Such a utilitarian definition is on the narrow end of the range of definitions presented by the authors consulted. By contrast, Li gave a comprehensive definition that was all-inclusive:

> A feasibility study can be described as a logical, systematic, and well-documented approach to solving a problem or analyzing a proposal. More aptly, it may be defined as a critical investigation conducted to establish the practical or economic justification, or both, of an idea, standard, technique, software, or hardware. The concept is not new, it has been applied to different problems in varying degrees for many years. Properly executed it becomes a critical examination for determining an organization's needs, and the cost-benefit relationships of existing and proposed approaches. [119:125]

From the current available literature on management information system design, an intensive search revealed that thirty of these authors specifically referred to the feasibility study phase of conceptual design in some detail. Table 1 contains the results of a breakdown for the ideas of these thirty authors. This tabulation was made from the pertinent factors that the authors felt should be included under the feasibility study phase of conceptual design.

Economic feasibility led the list of important factors to be included in a feasibility study. Sixty percent of the authors discussed both management involvement and the necessity for stating objectives. A study of the present system was included for this phase by approximately forty-seven percent of the authors, but many of those not included here did discuss a study of the present system under one of the other subdivisions. Technical feasibility and a study of the constraints were the topics for development by forty-three percent. After the first five topics, the percentages dropped drastically, with only seventeen percent covering a consideration of alternatives and a mere thirteen percent discussing operational or time feasibility.

Thirty percent of the authors listed all three of the top factors as being vital to an effective feasibility study. Particularly significant is the fact that twenty-three authors, or seventy-seven percent, listed at least two of the top three factors as being critical. With regard to the first four factors in the table, four authors (thirteen percent) discussed all four items, while fifty-seven percent listed three or more of the top four. Such unanimity among writers in the field evidenced the thinking concerning these various facets and their relative importance during the feasibility study.

When these factors were considered over the time span from 1966 through the 1976 publications, it was shown that three of these items were presented all the way through. These factors were: economic feasibility,

Table 1. Factors to Be Included in a Feasibility Study.

Factor	Percent Discussing Factor
Economic feasibility	83%
Management involvement	60%
Statement of objectives	60%
Study of present system	47%
Technical feasibility (study of constraints)	43%
Consideration of alternatives	17%
Operational or time feasibility	13%

management involvement, and a study of the old system. Particularly note-worthy was the fact that timewise, nine of the seventeen authors who listed a "statement of objectives" as a pertinent factor wrote either in 1975 or in 1976. Likewise, nine of the thirteen who listed "technical feasibility" published in those two years. These presentations reflected the growing awareness during this period of business in general, and especially management publications, of the necessity for emphasizing planning for the future. Furthermore, they also substantiated the trend toward the system approach, which called for beginning with a study of the objectives of a business.

Another especially interesting revelation from this study was that a 1967 article by R. George Glaser had been used to epitomize the heart of a feasibility study. In his article, "Are You Working on the Right Problem?" Glaser suggested that the feasibility study should give management the answer to three problems:

1. Can the job be done? – a technical question.

2. Should the job be done? – an economic question.

3. Will the system work? – an operational question. [76]

At least three of the authors use recognizable versions of this approach to feasibility, while many of the others presented variations of this theme as a catchy way to outline the requirements of a feasibility study [57, 114, 119].

Phase Two: Requirements Analysis

Although the term "requirements analysis" *per se* was not used by all of the authors studied, the essential idea of discovering business information needs was covered in most instances. Thomas Prince described this phase as an attempt "to understand the diverse objectives served by the business activities, because these diverse objectives are indicative of the basic requirements for information that the management system must satisfy" [150:137]. Perry Rosove listed the following purposes of this phase: "to determine why the system is needed, to identify the system users, and to define their information needs" [162:91]. He further emphasized that "The goals and objectives must be transformed into a set of operational requirements before design work can begin" [162:67].

As with the definition for feasibility study, the authors presented here a wide range of ideas, with some giving a narrow definition and others conveying an all-encompassing one. Robert Head gave a simple but lucid definition: "The needs of the prospective users of the system are surveyed and documented, and the objectives and outputs of the system defined" [87:99]. Exemplary of the in-depth definitions was that of Krauss:

> Requirements analysis begins with gaining a thorough knowledge of the business functions that are of concern. Included will be an understanding of management's objectives, underlying philosophy, attitude toward innovation and change, responsibilities, and plans for the future. [114:70]

For this phase also, the vital factors to be included in a study of requirements have been tabulated with the accompanying percentages in table 2. A study of the present system was discussed by an overwhelming ninety percent of the authors. Contrasted with this was the forty-seven percent attributed to the study of the system during the feasibility phase. Both user involvement and a study of information needs were given a high seventy percent inclusion. After this, the items discussed were not as unanimously covered. Although forty-seven percent of the writers discussed limits to cost, only twenty-three percent mentioned response time as being relevant and a mere seventeen percent discussed the necessity for system flexibility.

Especially notable from the data for table 2 was the fact that only three of the thirty authors consulted excluded a study of the present system from the requirements analysis phase. Such unanimity among these authorities in the MIS field further emphasized the importance of an investigation of the present system.

User involvement was also high on the list of the necessary steps for this phase, with seventy percent of the writers giving it special attention. Compare that percentage with the sixty percent rating found for management involvement during the feasibility study. Apparently writers felt that involvement of manager-users was even more important during the require-

Table 2.   Factors to Be Included in a
Requirements Analysis.

Factor	Percent Discussing Factor
Study of present system	90%
User involvement	70%
Study of information needs	70%
Limits to cost	47%
Response time	23%
System flexibility	17%

ments analysis. Running "neck-and-neck" in significance with user involvement was the necessity for studying information needs of a company. Twenty-one out of the thirty authors gave particular emphasis to this characteristic of requirement analysis.

A sharp drop in agreement was noted after the first three facets were listed. Such lack of commonality may be attributable to the various classification categories used for the conceptual design of a MIS. In his 1969 book, Sherman Blumenthal discussed different means of classification [23:91–92]. Such variation in the categories of the design development carried over for other authors who wrote after 1969. Although many of these writers used the term "requirement analysis," several employed the phrase as an all-inclusive, catch-all term. In numerous writings, the discussion of requirements analysis really shaded into the next phase—system specifications. Joel Ross emphasized this tendency by stating: "These steps in design are not separate and distinct. Indeed, most of them are along a continuum, shade into each other, overlap, and are recycled" [163].

Since twenty-seven of the thirty authors consulted highlighted the necessity for studying the present system, the reader should not be surprised to learn that there was no difference when these factors were considered over the 1966–1976 time-span. Inclusion of both user involvement and the need for studying information requirements likewise was scattered through the entire eleven years. Four of the five authors advocating the need for including system flexibility wrote from 1970 on, and six of the seven favoring response time also wrote after 1969.

Because such a large percentage of the writers discussed the top three items, it was not surprising that sixteen of the thirty (fifty-three percent) included all three of the items as being an integral part of requirements analysis. Furthermore, twenty-four of the thirty authors incorporated two or more of the first three categories in the pertinent factors for this phase. Nine of the thirty included all of the top four categories, while nineteen of the thirty listed at least three of the top four. The reputation of the writers consulted, as well as their work in the information systems field, further emphasized the importance of these factors during the requirements analysis phase.

Phase Three: System Specification

As a division of the overall conceptual design study, the term "system specification" was not specifically mentioned by all of the thirty authors. In fact, ten of the thirty did not treat this facet separately, two of the others covered it in a cursory manner, and one relegated it to a coverage of specifications for computer facilities alone.

With the term "system specification," identification varied from author to author, as was the case with many of the other definitions. One of the better definitions was presented by Li: "System specifications are prepared which spell out the functions the new system will achieve for the user" [119:118]. Several authors [50, 77] divided this category into three self-explanatory parts: performance specifications, design specifications, and system specifications. Explaining this division, Marvin Gore and John Stubbe stated:

> The Design Specification evolves from the Performance Specification, and the System Specification evolves from the Design Specification. And since these . . . are the only measurable evidence that progress is being made toward the creation of a useful . . . end-product, it is not possible to manage the life-cycle process without them. [77:19]

John Shaw and William Atkins considered this phase to be more technical. Evidence of their thinking was shown in the statement: "This activity gets its name from the specifications that will be developed[:] . . . more detailed preparation of programming specifications, hardware configuration planning, hardware specifications, communications network specifications . . ." [171:142]. Using an appropriate analogy, Jerome Kanter remarked that system specifications should be developed along the same line as engineering specifications for a specific piece of equipment [103:53].

Up to this point in the conceptual design of a management information system, activities described were largely nontechnical. With the "system specification" phase, analysis and descriptions moved to a middle level of technicality. Specifically, emphasis was on how operations would be performed, without descending to minute detail.

Several of the authors attempted to delineate the differences between system requirements and system specifications. One such explanation was that of Gore and Stubbe: "Whereas the Design Specification is a built-to specification, the System Specification is an as-built specification. It is the major reference document for all personnel who will use, maintain, or operate the computer-based business system" [77:350]. Another explanation for the difference was given by Shaw and Atkins: "System Requirements is a heavily user-oriented activity. . . . Studies deal almost entirely with the user organization" [171:32].

The classical argument as to which of these phases should come first was brought up by several writers, with some of them saying that the system design phase should precede the systems requirements phase. Along with Henry C. Lucas [122], Robert Head [87:129] felt that the design should come before specifications. Robert Murdick and Joel Ross [135:308] also presented specifications in this light, as did Ross [163:249].

For the seventeen remaining authors who devoted specific coverage to "system specification," the main topics of discussion were as listed in table 3.

Because of the lack of unanimity in definition and in coverage under the definition, the accumulated knowledge for this table was much less indicative of the thinking of the writers consulted. Across the board, all of the writers who discussed output followed that discussion by advocating a study of both input specifications and the flow of data through the organization. Because this phase was considered by many authors as being a more technical level than the system requirements phase, only six of the seventeen delineating this specific category mentioned user involvement. However, all of the others had at some place in their writing discussed the need for management-user active involvement and cooperation.

Although the idea was implicit in much of what the authors wrote, only three explicitly discussed the fact that the system specifications stage should be a stage for developing requirements. Such an idea, though, was inferred in the discussions stating that inputs, outputs, and data flow needed to be studied. Therefore, absence of specific mention was not necessarily indicative of the authors' thinking concerning the importance of developing requirements. In fact, some of the writers actually defined system specifications as being synonymous with developing requirements. Others may have felt that such a concept was so obvious that explicit coverage was not required.

When one sets up categories for breaking down the overall conceptual design, there is always the possibility that ideas have been overlooked. Furthermore, it is difficult to place bounds on creative thinking and to attempt to make the ideas of other authors fit into a particular mold. Therefore, this particular category's breakdown may not be as indicative of the real thinking of the thirty authors, as were the first two phases. In those

Table 3.   Factors to Be Included in
System Specification.

Factor	Percent Discussing Factor
Study of output	77%
Input specifications	77%
Study of data flow	77%
User involvement	35%
Developing requirements	18%

first two categories, authors almost universally designated the top characteristics. Furthermore, these writers displayed general agreement as to what
ideas should be included in each phase. No such agreement was evident for
the system specification phase.

Phase Four: System Design

Division of the conceptual design of a MIS into arbitrary phases was only to
make the discussion manageable. Actually, one would have a great deal of
difficulty in determining just exactly where one phase ended and the other
began. These were all meshed together, overlapping, and inextricably interwoven. Yet for the purpose of this research report, certain characteristics
were more important during one phase than another, so these were the
characteristics that were given emphasis.

Rosove expressed an idea which must be constantly considered
throughout the study of conceptual design of a management information
system. The findings of this research should be considered in the light of
Rosove's idea.

The use of the term "phase" in the context of system development should be qualified.
Only at a high level of abstraction can we assert that there are five (or eight) distinguish-
able phases of development and that they represent a logical and temporal sequence. In
some cases, the primary process within a phase which gives that phase its name, such as
requirements or design, is also an activity or function which is performed in other phases
as well. The system requirements, for example, must be determined before the initial
design activity, but the determination of requirements does not terminate at any specific
phase. Throughout the course of the development of a system, old requirements are
constantly undergoing refinement while more detailed requirements are being generated.
[162:18]

In this phase, the problem evolved around whether one referred to the overall process from the feasibility study through the implementation, or to the ingredient of the process termed "detailed design" by Murdick and Ross. In order to fit the schema depicted in the introduction, "detailed design" was the classification considered for this research report. Delineating the difference, Murdick and Ross remarked that "once the critical decision — the selection of the gross design — has been made, the detailed work is conducted to develop the operational and information systems in detail" [135:422].

Depending on their approach, some authors covered a number of the characteristics included here while others completely omitted particular items. However, so many factors were involved in the discussion of the design of an information system that omission probably was dependent on which factor was being emphasized. Several authors who omitted one or more of the previously discussed facets gave priority treatments to factors not relevant to this research report.

Many of the classifications were rather arbitrary, but a central theme seemed to permeate the discussions of system design. One of the earlier writers in this area was Sherman C. Blumenthal, who was recognized as a noted authority even though his work was published posthumously and was not entirely complete. Instead of using the term "system design," Blumenthal employed the words "framework for systems development." He explained that the more detailed level within the framework should be considered to be system design [23:61].

For the system design phase, Kanter presented a simplified definition: "The purpose of the design is to satisfy the systems requirements in the most efficient manner and at the lowest possible cost." Then, Kanter stated that the total information system should be broken down into small units which become meaningful and manageable subsystems [103:3]. Perhaps a more descriptive definition was given by Burch and Strater, who discussed the idea that this phase answered question about *how* the system should be developed to meet requirements. These authors then commented: "Systems design can be defined as the drawing, planning, sketching, or arranging of many separate elements into a viable, unified whole" [35].

As with the previous phases of conceptual design of a management information system, for this phase it was difficult to pinpoint the time when analysis ended and designing began. Several authors [4, 26] highlighted this fact, while M. J. Alexander lucidly described the idea:

> In most cases there will be no sharp demarcation between the completion of the analysis phase and the beginning of the design phase. . . . During the second stage . . . the systems

analyst will put together his bits and pieces of knowledge about the existing information system into a framework for an advanced one. [4:127]

An idea recurring in several of these writings was that design had often just occurred, with no formal planning. In his classic article, "Blueprint for MIS," William M. Zani remarked: "Traditionally, management information systems have not really been designed at all. They have been spun off as by-products of the process of automating or improving existing systems" [209:400]. Echoing this sentiment, Richard Brightman mentioned that design had not been formally instigated in some firms, but that often systems just "happened." Brightman further explained that a primary reason for lack of planning was the pressure of getting the job done—taking care of today's pressing problem and not giving much thought to future requirements [29:28].

A word found to be synonymous with "design" was that of "creativity." Taking the easy way out, some authors discussed design by stating that it was a creative effort and therefore not simple to define. As requirements for the design phase, Murdick and Ross listed broad thinking, experience, and creativity [135:446]. In the same vein, Robert Thierauf referred to design as being the "most creative phase" of the entire conceptual design [186:521]. Similar ideas were presented by Krauss and Donald Heany. Krauss stated that "more creative energy may be consumed in design than in any other stage" [114:105]. Discussing the requirements for the design phase, Heany proposed that a need existed for "unconventional, imaginative thinking in systems design" [88:60].

Another interesting finding was that the term "synthesis" was used by various authors while describing the design phase. Kanter described the purpose of the synthesis phase as one of putting the pieces together again, "retaining what can be salvaged and replacing what can not" [103:3]. Other references to the idea of synthesis were those of Gordon Davis [57:218] and Heany [88:73].

An appropriate summary statement for the concepts discussed for the design phase was found in these words from Heany: "The end result . . . is a conviction about how to proceed, a *general* idea as to what the major elements of a new information system might be, how they are related, and what other information systems interact" [88:65].

This study condensed the major facets in each of these phases for conciseness and quick appraisal. Actually, a one-sentence description for these factors was not sufficient, because a great deal of detail could be given for each division. However, the proposed plan was to present an overview, without concentrating on too much detail. For that reason, the vital factors involved in the system design phase have been reduced to simple phrases, as evidenced by table 4.

The five items listed in table 4 were the primary ideas discussed under the systems design phase. Since identifying and considering information needs are logical prerequisites of system design, the reader should not be surprised that this facet was given one hundred percent coverage by the thirty authors. Running closely behind were the importance of user support and the necessity for building control into the design itself. Each of these factors was mentioned by twenty-five of the thirty authors consulted.

Because "data base" and "integrated systems" have become pertinent "buzz words" when management information systems are discussed, almost all of the authors included at least these terms in their coverage of system design. However, many of the references were simply definitions of the concept or forecasts of what the future may hold. Eight of the thirty authors (twenty-seven percent) merely defined the term "data bases" and described how integrated data bases might be feasible in the future. Another four (thirteen percent) of the writers made no mention whatsoever of the data base concept. A similar percentage applied to the discussion of an integrated system, with five authors completely ignoring the idea and three only mentioning integrated systems as a future possibility. Five of the authors made no mention of integrated systems, but did use the idea of modular systems.

Interestingly, time did not influence the presentations of the authors. Both the concept of an integrated system and that of a data base were discussed during the period 1967 through 1976. What was especially surprising was that two of the authors who published in 1975 and one of the 1976 authors did not even give a cursory coverage of these factors. At this writing, data bases and integrated systems both seem much more feasible than in 1966, when authors omitted them from coverage.

Another pertinent fact that should be highlighted was the commonality of the writings for the design phase. Here, as opposed to the diversity of opinions or complete omissions of the system specifications phase, the writers reached agreement on the importance of needs identification, built-in control, and user support. Such significance was identified from 1966 through 1976.

Phase Five: Coding and Programming

Perhaps the choice of words for this stage was misleading, and "programming" would be a better designation. At any rate, regardless of what the authors labeled this stage, their definitions for the most part implied "programming."

Table 4.   Factors to Be Included in System Design.

Factor	Percent Discussing Factor
Identifying and considering information needs	100%
User support	83%
Built-in control	83%
Data base structure	60%
Integrated system	57%

Heany [88:237] was one of the few writers who actually used the term "coding" and then defined and discussed the term. The fact that his book was the oldest one consulted (1966) may account for the semantic difference. In 1966, "coding" may have meant "programming," or at least may have encompassed a larger aspect than the term did in 1976. In this current period when data bases are the vogue and a data base is established by working up standard "codes," another entirely different connotation has been given the term. According to Heany, "coding" meant "writing instructions for a sequence of computer operations" [88:237].

Many of the more recent writers did not include this phase of conceptual design in their discussions. They probably felt that competent people could handle this phase once the actual design had been conceived, or they may have felt that the programming phase was an "assumed" factor. Portraying the broader interpretation, Shaw and Atkins delineated the difference:

> Programming is the skill of expressing generalized system requirements and logical functions in specific, machine-compatible terms. This is done through the rendering of generalized objectives into specific instructions, or coding, which control computer performance. [171:201]

As with previously discussed phases, here also semantic differences appeared in the literature. While a few authors referred to "coding" as the actual procedure involved with giving numerical "codes" to various classes of data, most of the authors described writing computer programs as the principal activity for this phase. Because "coding" *per se* may be an "assumed" factor when one writes about conceptual design, eight of the thirty authors ignored this facet completely. A great deal of unanimity was discovered among the remaining twenty-two who discussed this stage in conceptual design, as indicated by table 5.

Table 5.   Factors to Be Included in
Coding and Programming.

Factor	Percent Discussing Factor
Standardization	86%
Team approach	82%
Accompanied by documentation	77%
Modularity	73%

Standardization was the factor that appeared to be of paramount importance to those writers discussing programming. Nineteen of the twenty-two (eighty-seven percent) included this facet. The team approach to programming was mentioned as being vital by eighteen of the twenty-two authors. Such coverage depicted the fact that the systems approach with involvement of both user-management and programmers was considered fundamental to the success of this phase. Next on the list of indispensible factors was the idea that programming should be accompanied by documentation. Seventeen of the twenty-two writers (seventy-seven percent) felt that documentation to accompany the programs was a vital aspect.

The last factor given any common coverage by the twenty-two writers studied was the need for programming in modules. The basic discussion here was that these modules would be easier to program and then they could later be integrated into a workable system. Several other ideas were presented by a few of the writers, but no universality of coverage appeared. Therefore, these factors were not included in the discussion. As previously mentioned, no attempt was made to distinguish between the "top-down" and "bottom-up" approach to integration.

Omission of the discussion concerning coding and programming followed no particular time sequence. Of the eight authors who made no mention of these terms, one wrote in 1966, one in 1969, three in 1970, two in 1975, and one in 1976. However, three of the eight (thirty-eight percent) wrote in the last two of those years, while six of them (seventy-five percent) published in the last six. Such figures could indicate the decreasing emphasis or preoccupation with programming as more and more proficiency was gained in this area.

Because of the high percentages in all of these areas, the reader should expect maximum coverage of these factors. Actually, thirteen of the twenty-two authors (fifty-nine percent) included all four of the categories in their lists of imperatives for a successful MIS. Furthermore, sixty-eight percent covered at least three of the top four in their discussions.

Phase Six: Testing

For this particular phase, the term itself was self-explanatory, so that no actual definition need be given for "testing." However, the extent of the testing was found to be an arbitrary criterion. Henry Lucas discussed the idea that testing should be all encompassing and should include "verification of the basic logic of each program and verification that the entire system works properly" [122:188]. A particularly clear and concise discussion of testing was made by Joel Ross: "The design can be tested to see whether it yields appropriate outputs to meet the previously defined objectives and information needs" [163:256].

Rather than devote space to defining "testing," many writers used this phase as a vehicle for discussing why testing should be carried out. Others pointed out the extreme importance of testing, although they felt it had often been shortchanged. Leonard Krauss gave such a comment: "The eventually crippling side effects of a poorly managed testing phase can build to a point where the company's operations may be in jeopardy" [114:250]. In the same vein, Krauss continued his discussion by listing seven major types of tests he considered mandatory for an effective MIS. A similar idea was advanced by Li in his statement "Testing is vital to the success of a system, and therefore, is worthy of careful scrutiny" [119:210]. Shaw and Atkins advocated an excellent analogy for this phase by comparing the testing phase to a shakedown cruise for a new ship. In carrying this theme further, they commented that projects should not be considered "seaworthy" until all necessary tests had been made [171:221].

The actual presentation of ideas about the testing phase has been tabulated in table 6. Of the thirty authors, eight did not include testing in their discussions of conceptual design. One of the possible reasons for this omission may be that the writers did not feel testing was relevant. Another explanation may be that writers considered testing to be implicitly assumed as a necessary function for any viable information system.

Paramount among the ideas covered for the testing phase were both planning for testing and measurement through testing. The importance of these two facets was emphasized by the fact that twenty-one of the twenty-two writers included these ideas in their essential list. The remarkable thing here was that one author did *not* mention these factors as vital characteristics for testing. Planning for implementation tests and measuring the effectiveness and efficiency of an MIS have become such an integral part of successful management systems that they are almost prerequisites.

Table 6.   Factors to Be Included in Testing.

Factor	Percent Discussing Factor
Measurement through testing	95%
Planning for testing	95%
Parallel testing	91%
Modular, integrative testing	82%
Independently generated test data	73%
Top management involvement	68%

Next in order of priority, according to these authors, was the need for parallel testing of the system. In the "world" of management information systems, parallel testing has become almost synonymous with testing itself. Many people currently working with such systems would feel that an omission of the parallel portion of testing was almost ludicrous.

Eighteen of the twenty-two writers highlighted the idea that testing should be both modular and integrative. Theirs was the traditional approach, probably attributable to the "state of the art" at the time many of them published. Such coverage implied that the systems should be tested in parts (modules) and then as an integrated whole. An intriguing point was that some authors who published in 1968 and 1969 presented these ideas of modular and integrative testing, while two 1976 writers did not. Designing systems in modules and then integrating the modules supposedly was a relatively new idea, yet the authors included these factors in 1968.

Although fifteen of the twenty-two writers thought top management should become involved during the testing phase, seven of the twenty-two did not cover such participation. Somewhere in their discussions of management information systems, many of the same authors had previously mentioned the need for top management involvement throughout the entire system design. Therefore, a possibility existed that these authors felt specific mention of management involvement was not necessary for the testing phase discussion.

Sixteen of the twenty-two specifically mentioned that the test data used for running the tests should be independently generated. The gist of this idea was that someone other than the programmers should compose the test data. Improved testing resulted when test data came from more than one source, since the possibilities were much greater for eradicating errors before actual operation began.

As with the previously discussed phases, the writers presented a number of other ideas under the testing phase. However, no one facet was given sufficient coverage to warrant inclusion in the list.

Phase Seven: Documentation

The consensus of the authors was that documentation should be an essential part of the entire conceptual design. Although some writers referred to documentation as being tedious, time-consuming, and boring [107, 119, 127], all agreed that documentation was a necessity in management system design. Explaining that methods for accumulating business information were once so simple that the steps could be memorized, Gerald Silver and Joan Silver then compared those prior days with current business operations:

> Today, however, the complexity and sophistication of modern business systems dictate a more reliable method of describing a system. . . . [D]ocumentation . . . involves creating, collecting, organizing, storing, citing, and disseminating documents containing information relating to the structure and details of a system. [174:209]

A major portion of the writing in the documentation phase was devoted to listing the prerequisites for good documentation or to explaining why documentation was so often completely disregarded or at least slighted. Li highlighted this idea with his pertinent statement that documentation was "one of the most neglected aspects" of system design. He further reiterated this thought by discussing how most businesses who did slight the documentation phase always felt that there would be time to catch up tomorrow, although "tomorrow never seemed to come" [119:244].

Joseph Kelly sounded an ominous but factual note when he stated that "failure to ensure that the programming work has been adequately documented will extract a heavy price from the organization" [107:492]. Although this particular reference was to the programming part of documentation, such a warning could easily be applied to the entire range of documentation necessary for system design.

Summing up what other authors wrote about documentation, Silver and Silver listed guidelines for preparing documentation and stated:

> The usefulness of documentation is only as good as the time and effort expended on its preparation. Hurriedly written or incomplete documentation has limited value. Some documentation is so tersely written, or explained in jargon so technical that it can only be understood by someone intimately familiar with the system. This defeats the basic purpose of documentation. [174:492]

Of the thirty authors consulted, six did not discuss documentation. An interesting fact was that all six of these authors wrote before 1971. Two other authors were excluded from the count because they omitted all of the facets of documentation except documenting data bases and information flow. These two writers have become prolific authors and widely recognized experts in the management information field almost from its inception. Consequently, one might feel that they considered documentation to be an "assumed" feature of the design phase. Their omission of the documentation of other factors was interpreted to mean that the factors not discussed were so essential they did not need specific mention.

In light of the previous discussion, then, only twenty-two authors were included in the computations presented in table 7.

The documentation phase of conceptual system design had wider agreement among the writers than did any of the other phases. Notice the complete agreement for the top three factors: documentation should be complete, objectives should be included in documentation, and information flow should be documented. All but one of the writers advocated that documentation should be a continuous procedure. In addition, none of the factors received a percentage below eighty-six percent.

All of the writers felt that documentation should be complete, while many described in detail the components of complete documentation [48, 64, 107, 171, 186]. These writers unanimously reported that documenting objectives and the flow of information for the business should be included in complete documentation. That documentation should not only be complete, but should also be accomplished on a continuous basis, was the factor that was highlighted by twenty-one of the twenty-two authors.

Clarity in documentation was thought to be of paramount importance by nineteen of the twenty-two writers, while the documentation of data bases was discussed by a similar number of authors. Particularly interesting was the fact that the three authors who did not cover documenting data bases wrote in 1968, 1971, and 1972. Of the writers consulted, all who have published since 1972 gave extensive coverage to the necessity for documenting data bases.

Phase Eight: Implementation

The final phase in conceptual design was really the culmination of the entire project. Often implementation has been described as the actual "live" operation of the system, with a list of the potential problems and steps to avoid. A terse but lucid definition was presented by Murdick and Ross: "The output of design work is a set of specifications, implementation is the conversion of these specifications into a working system" [135:422].

Several authors indicated that they felt that the implementation phase was not relevant to conceptual design because this phase involved the actual

Table 7.   Factors to Be Included in Documentation.

Factor	Percent Discussing Factor
Completeness in documentation	100%
Documenting objectives	100%
Documenting information flow	100%
Continuous documentation	95%
Clarity in documentation	86%
Data base documentation	86%

Table 8.   Factors to Be Included in Implementation.

Factor	Percent Discussing Factor
Planning and control	100%
Evaluation of the system	100%
Parallel operation	95%
Capacity for handling problems	95%
Preparation for users	95%
Top management involvement	77%

doing rather than the planning. However, a completely planned system should be one which also included planning for implementation. This idea was the connotation for implementation which this research report addressed.

Of the thirty authors, five completely omitted a discussion of implementation, while three gave the term a cursory treatment. Their superficial coverage mentioned that the phase did exist. Then, these three writers made broad, all-inclusive statements worded as catch-all phrases designed to cover all aspects of implementation, without including any of the specifics.

The results of the ideas from the remaining twenty-two authors have been depicted in table 8.

Unanimous coverage was given to the importance of planning and control and to evaluating the management information system during the implementation phase. One would expect both of these factors to be given priority, since each was practically essential to a successful system. Near conformity was also portrayed for the next three facets. Twenty-one of the twenty-two authors (ninety-five percent) advocated an implementation

Table 9.   Summary of Literature Findings for Factors Included in Eight
Phases of Conceptual Design.

Phase and Factor	Percent Including Factor
FEASIBILITY STUDY	
Economic feasibility	83%
REQUIREMENTS ANALYSIS	
Study of present system	90%
SYSTEM SPECIFICATIONS	
Study of output	76%
Input specifications	76%
Study of data flow	76%
SYSTEM DESIGN	
Identification & consideration of needs	100%
CODING & PROGRAMMING	
Standardization	86%
TESTING	
Measurement through testing	95%
Planning for testing	95%
DOCUMENTATION	
Complete	100%
Documenting objectives	100%
Documenting information flow	100%
IMPLEMENTATION	
Planning and control	100%
Evaluation of the system	100%

phase which prepared the users for the conversion. The same percentage
discussed the need for an implementation phase which had a capacity to
handle problems and included parallel operations. The only unexpected
result of this compilation was that not all of the authors specifically mentioned the need for top management involvement during the implementation phase. Although seventy-seven percent was a relatively high percentage, top management involvement has become so vital to the entire system
design that its omission by even a few authors was remarkable.

Summation of the Results

Under the feasibility study phase, economic feasibility was selected by a wide margin, with management involvement and a statement of objectives following. The requirements analysis phase highlighted the need for studying the present system, but also included the importance of user involvement and a study of information needs. Under the system specifications heading, the three items given equal coverage were study of output, input specifications, and study of data flow. Identifying and considering information needs were the topics given complete unanimity by the authors for the design phase. Standardization in coding was considered to be most vital to effective design, with the team approach to programming following in importance. Under testing, both measurement through testing and planning for testing were considered essential. For the documentation phase, three factors were discussed by all of the authors: completeness, documentation of objectives, and documentation of the information flow. Primary importance during the implementation phase was given to planning and control and to evaluating the system.

Table 9 capsules the findings of this chapter. In this table, each of the phases has been listed along with the top categories and accompanying percentages.

6

The Delphi Technique Applied to Phases of Conceptual Design

How 1976 opinions toward conceptual design of information systems compared with ideas from the published literature about the MIS field was the question addressed by chapter 5. The comparison was highlighted by obtaining ideas from well-known authors and practitioners in the MIS field. Chapter 7 discusses the same question as answered by typical authors and practitioners in the 1980s.

The invention and advance of computers made possible their application to large-scale information systems. In chapter 2, the evolution of computers as applied in business was chronicled. Chapter 3, in turn, discussed how the computer evolution affected the development of management information systems in the United States. Chapter 4 updated the computer applications to the present by listing many of the current concepts that have become popular since the microcomputer entered the business scene. These chapters were primarily background for chapter 5, where the writings of noted authors in the MIS field were discussed. The purpose of chapter 5 was to delineate ideas of well-known authors in the MIS field toward conceptual design of management information systems. Specifically, their thoughts in relation to the eight phases of conceptual design of such systems were summarized.

In chapter 6 the focal points are pertinent facets of the conceptual design of a management information system, according to the thinking of contemporary authors and practitioners. The Delphi technique is the vehicle for obtaining current opinions of these experts. Current thinking is then compared with concepts available from the published literature in the MIS field. From a combination of the available literature and ideas obtained through the Delphi method, a reasonably likely set of criteria for designing a management information system is determined. This chapter outlines the Delphi method, examines the concept of the Delphi technique, and then describes the particular study conducted. Finally, a summary of the study is presented.

General Discussion of the Delphi

Because it is a composite of expert opinions, the Delphi technique was selected for this research. In studying the conceptual design for large-scale information systems, this research report covered relevant literature in the management information systems field. Then, as a means of reinforcing or validating the criteria presented in MIS literature, the Delphi technique was employed to question a selected group of "experts" from the MIS field.

Since people working with management information systems comprised a homogeneous group, a small number of participants could be expected to yield excellent results. The original purpose of this Delphi study was to generate consensus on factors of importance in each of the phases of conceptual design. Toward that end, the results of the original Questionnaire #1 identified pertinent factors and included clarifications, supporting comments, or criticisms. Questionnaire #2 listed these factors obtained through the first mailing. Results of Questionnaire #2 gave a preliminary indication of priorities of the participants. The third and final questionnaire permitted the respondents to review prior responses and express their individual judgments as to the importance of each facet.

Present-day applications of the Delphi method have been lucidly described in a 1975 book written by Andre L. Delbecq, Andrew Van de Ven and David Gustafson. Benefits of using the Delphi technique, as listed in this book are:

> It provides closure for the study.
>
> It suggests areas where diversity of judgment exists, but allows for the aggregation of judgment.
>
> It provides guidelines for future research and planning. [59:104]

All three of these benefits certainly accrued from the application of the Delphi technique to this research study. The effort of the participants was worthwhile, adding validity to the literature search of this book. Although priorities were aggregated by votes of participants, individual differences in judgment still existed. These differences are highlighted under the discussion of the third round. Several intriguing suggestions for future research and planning in the MIS field resulted from the comments and proposals of the participants. The entire Delphi study has been included in the appendix.

Description of Participants

Respondents or potential participants for the Delphi technique employed in this research were selected on the basis of either authorship in the field or extensive business practice in planning or designing management information systems. Because the research is heavily oriented toward the pertinent literature about MIS, more authors than practitioners were contacted. However, balance and depth were added by the opinions of three authorities whose companies were heavily involved in management information systems. The original thinking was that there might be differences between what writers and practitioners thought about MIS conceptual design.

Since the participants selected felt personally involved and had pertinent information to share, they were highly motivated to participate. This covered three of the requisites for respondents to a Delphi study. A fourth requirement was that the respondents feel the information would be valuable and accessible only through the Delphi study. Not only did these authorities have a deep interest in the problem, but they also contributed important knowledge or valuable experience.

Initial Contact of Respondents

For the original round of the Delphi, prominent writers and three authorities from major business firms were selected and asked to participate. The Delbecq, Van de Ven and Gustafson book mentioned above [59] suggested that these potential participants first be contacted by telephone. However, the time required for explanation of the method and purpose of this particular study was so lengthy, letters were first sent to participants. Then, where no response was made to the initial letter, telephone contacts were made.

Of the twenty people in the original group who were sent letters, fourteen agreed to participate. Such a large number of respondents may seem remarkable. However, these were all people with an interest in the MIS field and in any new developments concerning management information systems. As previously mentioned, one of the essential requirements of respondents was that they be highly motivated to participate. All twenty of the original group were selected on that basis.

Originally, the Delphi technique was designed to prevent domination by certain individuals since the participants remain anonymous. Such a method is truly more objective than a face-to-face encounter of the experts. Delbecq, Van de Ven and Gustafson further remarked in their book that "with a homogeneous group of people, ten to fifteen participants might be enough" [43:15]. Their discussion further explained that few new ideas could be expected to be generated from a larger number. The fourteen participants for this particular Delphi study, then, comprised an excellent group from which to obtain pertinent information concerning the phases of conceptual design for a management information system.

Delphi Study: Round One

When used to obtain a consensus of opinions of experts, the first round of the Delphi technique should be completely unstructured. The experts are asked a general question in such a way that their answers are strictly individual opinions. For this research, the first question simply asked the participants to name the factors which they felt were of highest importance for each of the eight phases of conceptual design. As presented to these experts, the question was an open-ended one, with the entire answer encompassing only one page. Such a short survey was to make the process appear to be easy and also to encourage conciseness and clarity in the answers.

The original questionnaire indicated no set pattern of development for these eight phases of conceptual design. The authorities questioned simply answered by giving factors which they felt should be included under each phase. In fact, the original questionnaire asked for *the one* factor which the participants felt was of paramount importance under each of these phases. However, many of the respondents listed more than one facet because they felt that several characteristics needed to be included.

Excellent response to the first questionnaire demonstrated the interest of the group of participants and their willingness to share pertinent information concerning management information systems. From this first questionnaire, one of the remarkable results was that the most detailed and lucid coverage came from one of the business respondents. This particular business representative had obviously divided the various phases among knowledgeable practitioners in his firm. The answers were then from people who were truly "experts" in each of the particular areas. Also of special interest was the revelation that the business practitioners were the ones who proposed using the latest techniques, such as Hierarchy-Input-Processing-Output programming, while such methods were not mentioned by the writers.

Twenty letters were mailed to the experts, with fourteen answering the first questionnaire. In listing these answers under the various categories, no particular importance was given to the order in which each of the facets was listed. For clarity and conciseness, ideas were arbitrarily classified into categories for the second mailing. The factors mentioned by the participants of Round One are shown in table 10, which contains the phases of conceptual design for a management information system.

Table 10.   Responses to the First Delphi Round.

I.   FEASIBILITY STUDY
        User Involvement
        Study of Current Information Flow
        Study of User Attitudes & Expectations
        Economic Feasibility
        Study of Present System
        Top Management Involvement
        Planning for Long Range

II.   REQUIREMENTS ANALYSIS
        Cost vs. Response Time
        Study of Needs
        User Involvement
        Study of Current System

III. SYSTEM SPECIFICATIONS
        Developing Requirements
        User Involvement
        Outputs
        Inputs
        Data Flow

IV.   SYSTEM DESIGN
        Integrated System
        Consideration of the Data Base
        User Support
        Identification & Consideration of Needs
        Method of Designing
        Built In Control

V.   CODING
        Modular
        Standardized
        Accompanied by Documentation
        Established Goals for Programmers
        Test Data Development
        Not Applicable to Conceptual Design
        Team Approach

Table 10.   (continued)

VI.   TESTING
          Parallel
          Independent Data Generation
          Modular & Integrative
          Not Relevant to Conceptual Design
          Top Management Involvement
          Measurement of System through Testing
          Planning

VII.   DOCUMENTATION
          Completeness
          Information Flow Documentation
          Data Base Documentation
          Documentation for User
          Objectives Documented
          Continuous Documentation

VIII.   IMPLEMENTATION
          User Preparation
          Top Management Support
          Not Relevant
          Capability for Handling Problems
          Parallel
          Phased Implementation
          Evaluation
          Planning and Control

Delphi Study: Round Two

The answers to Round One were tabulated under each of the eight phases, with the comments of the individual participants recorded. These responses were then categorized and accumulated. Where ideas were unique, these were expressed explicitly. Duplications, however, were avoided to keep the mailing from being too voluminous. For the second round, the respondents received a categorized group of factors under each of the eight phases. The condensed version sent to the respondents has been presented in table 10, with the detailed version in the appendix. To prevent the tabulation from influencing answers from the second round, factors listed by first-round participants were presented in the second mailing in no particular order.

Accompanying each of the phases were the pertinent comments sent in for the first round.

Respondents were asked to read the results of the first round, along with the comments from other experts in the MIS field. They were then asked to rank the factors listed in the order of importance as they saw them. Along with detailed coverage sheets of the results from the first round, each respondent received summary sheets. On these summary sheets, the participants were asked to give a ranking of the individual factors under each phase. In addition, these respondents were to add any comments which they felt pertinent to the discussion. Should they feel that important facets had been omitted from the original list for any of the phases, the participants were asked to include these in their responses.

Additional comments from the second round were especially interesting and enlightening. Several of the participants added factors under some of the phases, along with their reasons for including such facets. Other respondents discussed in detail their thinking about particular factors.

From the results of the second round, rankings of these experts were compiled. In order to give weight only to the items ranked, first place items were given a weight of five, second place items a weight of four, etc. The item with the highest composite score under each particular phase was considered to be the most important factor for that phase, as ranked by these participants.

These compiled results were then presented on both detail and summary sheets; this time, though, the resulting facets were listed in the order of their voted importance. The appendix contains a copy of both the detail and summary sheets resulting from the second round. Table 11 portrays the top two items for each of the eight phases, as selected by the Delphi participants. Particularly noteworthy was that user involvement stood out, in one form or another, among these priority items.

During the second round, participants added factors to seven of the eight categories, with the implementation phase being the only one where no new factors were suggested. These additional facets are presented in table 12 by category, in no particular order since each was suggested by only one respondent.

Delphi Study: Round Three

Along with the summary sheets described above, remarks from the second round of the Delphi were included with the detail sheets for each category. On both the detail and summary sheets, participants were given spaces to make additional remarks in the third round. The compiled results of the second mailing were sent to all the participants and they were asked once

Table 11.   Priority Items for Delphi Study by Phases.

I.   FEASIBILITY STUDY
      User Involvement
      Top Management Involvement

II.   REQUIREMENTS ANALYSIS
      User Involvement
      Study of (User) Needs

III. SYSTEM SPECIFICATIONS
      User Involvement
      Outputs

IV.   SYSTEM DESIGN
      Identification & Consideration of Needs
      Integrated System

V.   CODING
      Standardized
      Modular

VI.   TESTING
      Parallel
      Measurement of System through Testing

VII. DOCUMENTATION
      Documentation for User
      Completeness

VIII. IMPLEMENTATION
      User Preparation
      Capability for Handling Problems

---

again to rank the facets under each of the eight phases of conceptual design. After seeing what other experts thought, the respondents were given an opportunity to reconsider their individual rankings. A few changes were evidenced; that is, items ranked first for the second round were ranked differently under the third round.

Detailed comparisons of the results of the second and third questionnaires have been included for each of the eight phases of conceptual design. The composite results of both the second and third rounds are presented in the tables below. In addition to the composite results, the third-round selec-

Table 12.   Additional Factors Suggested in Round Two.

I.   FEASIBILITY STUDY
       Operational Feasibility
       Technical Feasibility

II.   REQUIREMENTS ANALYSIS
       Specify Short-run & Long-run Requirements
       Improve Control
       Limits to Cost
       Economic Analysis
       Improvement in Managerial Control
       Reports — Mode & Level of Aggregation

III.   SYSTEM SPECIFICATIONS
       System Chart
       File Design
       Data Coding System

IV.   SYSTEM DESIGN
       Hardware & Software
       Data Coding System

V.   CODING
       Integration of Code Numbers into a Total System
          of Codes

VI.   TESTING
       Preimplementation & Postimplementation Testing

VII.   DOCUMENTATION
       Standardized

---

tions have been divided into decisions by the practitioners and by the authors, simply for informative purposes. Often no difference existed at all between the choices of the authors and the practitioners, as indicated in the discussion of the phases. However, marked differences were occasionally evident among the two groups. Because the survey was weighted heavily toward the authors, their selection agreed with the composite group ratings more often than did the listings of the practitioners.

Delphi Study: Summary of Findings

Table 13 depicts the rankings for the feasibility study phase. This table, as well as the others in the summary, has two parts; the first is a comparison

Table 13.   Rankings for Feasibility Study Phase.

Factor	Composite Rankings		Group Rankings	
	Round 2	Round 3	Business	Authors
User Involvement	1	1	1	2
Top Management Involvement	2	1 (tie)	2	1
Economic Feasibility	3	3	—	3
Study of User Attitude & Expectations	4	—	—	4
Planning for the Long Range	5	4	3	4
Study of Current Information Flow	—	5	5	5

of the composite rankings for the second and third rounds of the Delphi mailing. An additional feature of each table is the division of the third round composite score into decisions by the business firms and the writers.

Both the writers and the practitioners were in near agreement on the first two categories under feasibility study—involvement of both user management and top management. Authors put much more emphasis on economic feasibility, while the practitioners highlighted long-range planning and the need to study user attitudes and expectations. Furthermore, unanimity on the importance of studying the current information flow was revealed by the results, as depicted by table 13.

For the requirements analysis phase, the participants reached a remarkable unanimous agreement. No deviation appeared between the second- and third-round selections or between the ratings of the practitioners and writers. The results of these rankings are depicted in table 14.

Under the third category, system specifications, the participants reached complete agreement on the most important facet, user involvement. The factor listed in the number two spot was nearly unanimously selected, with only the authors in Round Three giving this a third place rating. All groups agreed that data flow was fifth in importance under this phase, but the practitioners rated inputs third as compared to the composite for both rounds and the authors' rating of fourth. Note also that the practitioners put added emphasis on the importance of file design by giving that facet a rating of fourth, as shown in table 15.

Under the system design phase, rankings were the same for both the second and third round and for the authors for the first three facets listed. On the other hand, the practitioners simply switched first and second places

Table 14. Rankings for Requirements Analysis Phase.

Factor	Composite Rankings Round 2	Round 3	Group Rankings Business	Authors
User Involvement	1	1	1	1
Study of Needs	2	2	2	2
Study of Current System	3	3	3	3
Cost vs. Response Time	4	4	4	4
Specify Short-run & Long-run Requirements	—	5	5	5

Table 15. Rankings for System Specifications Phase.

Factor	Composite Rankings Round 2	Round 3	Group Rankings Business	Authors
User Involvement	1	1	1	1
Outputs	2	2	2	3
Developing Requirements	3	3	—	2
Inputs	4	4	3	4
Data Flow	5	5	5	5
File Design	—	—	4	—

by giving integrated systems preference over identification and consideration of needs. In this phase, the practitioners felt that user support should be third instead of receiving the fourth and fifth ratings of the other groups. Consideration of the data base was in the top five of all groups, but the practitioners gave this factor a lower rating than did the authors and the composite groupings, as table 16 indicates.

Another example of extraordinary agreement came from the rankings for the coding phase of conceptual design. Complete agreement was evidenced for the first four factors, with the only difference being in the fifth place listing.

Integration of code numbers into a total system of codes, a facet added as a result of the second round, was given a number five rating by the practitioners instead of the category of test data development which all

Table 16.   Rankings for System Design Phase.

Factor	Composite Rankings		Group Rankings	
	Round 2	Round 3	Business	Authors
Identification & Consideration of Needs	1	1	2	1
Integrated System	2	2	1	2
Consideration of the Data Base	3	3	4	3
Method of Designing	4	5	5	4
User Support	5	4	3	5

other groups ranked five. The complete listing for the coding phase is shown in table 17.

The testing phase revealed the most noticeable differences of any of the eight phases of conceptual design. The composite rankings for Rounds Two and Three and that of the writers gave parallel testing a number one rating, but the practitioners listed that factor as only in fifth place. To the practitioners, planning had top priority, as shown in table 18. For the second round of the Delphi, measurement of the system through testing was rated second. Evidently, on further consideration, the participants had a change of mind, because this facet was ranked no higher than fourth in the third round. Similarly, modular and integrative testing as a facet of the testing phase was moved up in the ratings from third to second. Independent data generation appeared to be more vital to the practitioners than to the writers, since the former ranked this factor third as compared to a fifth place rating by the latter.

A great deal of diversity appeared in the ratings under the documentation phase, although everyone questioned agreed that documentation was necessary to conceptual design. Part of the problem was undoubtedly derived from the actual wording used. Several writers made lucid, succinct comments to the effect that "completeness" was an integral part of all the other facets listed under the documentation phase. This marked difference especially appeared in the top categories, where documentation for the user was ranked from first through fourth. Data base documentation was not listed in the top five items for the second round, but was included by all of the groupings in the third round. In addition, the fourth place rating given to documentation of objectives was completely ignored by all raters in the third round, as shown in table 19.

Table 17. Rankings for the Coding Phase.

Factor	Composite Rankings		Group Rankings	
	Round 2	Round 3	Business	Authors
Standardized	1	1	1	1
Modular	2	2	2	2
Accompanied by Documentation	3	3	3	3
Established Goals for Programmers	4	4	4	4
Test Data Development	5	5	–	5
Integration of Code Numbers into a Total System of Codes	–	–	5	–

Table 18. Rankings for the Testing Phase.

Factor	Composite Rankings		Group Rankings	
	Round 2	Round 3	Business	Authors
Parallel Testing	1	1	5	1
Measurement of System through Testing	2	4	4	4
Modular & Integrative	3	2	2	2
Planning	4	3	1	3
Independent Data Generation	5	5	3	5

Differences were also evident for the rankings under implementation, the eighth phase of conceptual design. All groupings agreed that user preparation was of utmost importance, but the other four rankings varied widely, as is depicted in table 20.

Although capability for handling problems was ranked second in importance under this phase during Round Two, the authors did not place this facet in the top five for the third round. Likewise, evaluation with a third place rating in Round Two was ignored for the composite Round Three with only the authors ranking it fourth. A remarkable fact was the climb in importance for planning and control from fourth to second for all

Table 19.   Rankings for the Documentation Phase.

Factor	Composite Rankings		Group Rankings	
	Round 2	Round 3	Business	Authors
Documentation for User	1	2	1	4
Completeness	2	1	3	1
Continuous Documentation	3	3	2	2
Objectives Documented	4	—	—	—
Information Flow Documentation	5	4	5	3
Data Base Documentation	—	5	4	5

Table 20.   Rankings for the Implementation Phase.

Factor	Composite Rankings		Group Rankings	
	Round 2	Round 3	Business	Authors
User Preparation	1	1	1	1
Capability for Handling Problems	2	5	4	—
Evaluation	3	—	—	4
Planning & Control	4	2	2	2
Top Management Support	5	3	—	3
Parallel	—	—	5	—
Phased Implementation	—	4	3	5

groupings. Only the practitioners considered parallel implementation worth one of the five rankings, while top management support was rated by all groups except the practitioners. Even though phased implementation was not included in the composite top five for Round Two, this facet received a remarkable amount of recognition for all of the Round Three ratings.

Suggestions for Further Research

Although the original terminology for each of the categories came from the participants themselves, a great deal of overlap was evident. In addition, semantic differences which accompany a dynamic field such as management information systems often left interpretation of terms to the particular participant. An example of such differences was encountered with the feasibility study phase. Several respondents felt that the categories of "user involvement" and "study of user attitudes and expectations" were identical, while other participants specifically listed these as being two separate categories. Since specific definitions are yet to be established in the management information systems field, misinterpretation of meaning often resulted.

From the pertinent comments and suggestions that many of the categories overlapped, the concept evolved that further research should be made into applicable terms for describing the facets under each of these phases of conceptual design. Vocabulary and definition of terms both play a vital part in the designation of factors for each of these phases. By explicitly spelling out the interpretation given these terms, perhaps another study might reduce duplication and overlap.

Lucid comments from several of the noted authors concerned the eight phases themselves. As previously mentioned, these were arbitrarily chosen to depict the conceptual design of a management information system. No unanimous agreement among writers existed as to the number of phases to be included or to the specific titles of these phases. One author questioned the order of the phases used for this study, commenting that the design phase should precede the specification phase. Another well-known authority felt that several of the specific eight phases were not relevant to conceptual design itself. These suggestions were epitomized by the question from one expert: "Why not have experts rate the major phases as well?" Utilizing such an idea, another study might be made in which the initial Delphi questionnaire asked the experts simply to list the major phases of conceptual design of a management information system.

A Look Forward

The next chapter highlights results of a "revisit" using the Delphi technique. Comparison is made between the findings of the original study and a follow-up in the mid-1980s. Then, three following chapters depict the application of both the pertinent characteristics developed from the Delphi study and similar factors found through the literature search. These facets are applied to actual business systems, and activities both with the companies and with the systems are brought up-to-date. Chapter 8 reveals how the Bell Telephone System developed the BISCUS/FACS management information system. Specifically, this system is examined in light of the guidelines developed. The transition of the system during and since the Bell System divestiture is then examined.

Chapter 9 depicts the development of management information systems for American Airlines, with an update on operation of this system since deregulation of the airlines. Chapter 10 studies Weyerhaeuser, with particular focus on the facets found in the Delphi study and in the literature search. Finally, a comparison of the literature findings and those resulting from the Delphi method is presented in the concluding chapter. This comparison includes summarizing remarks as to applications of these guidelines to the actual business systems studied, along with current concepts and prevalent ideas concerning the systems development life cycle as of the mid-1980s.

7

The Delphi Revisited

Background

The original Delphi study was conducted in order to gain opinions about the important factors of each stage of the systems development life cycle in the design of a management information system. Eight phases in the design were used as a "given."

In the mid-1980s, systems analysis and design is no longer thought of as "black magic" or an artistic ability that one either has or does not have. Instead, during the ten years since the original research was conducted, many practitioners have laboriously developed and refined methods of designing and analyzing successful systems. During this period, through the trial-and-error method, these designers have discovered that systems analysis and design *can* be taught. Out of the efforts expended by both academicians and practitioners in the study and application of the systems development life cycle, many changes have come. A number of these are reflected in the responses discussed on the following pages.

In the ensuing ten years between the original Delphi study and the current research, many changes in the opinions of the "experts" can be expected. The original participants were contacted and asked to give their current opinions about the systems life cycle. Although not all of them answered, a few new opinions were obtained. Two participants gave their opinions of the current state of the art rather than giving specific answers to the first phase of the Delphi. Such remarks, or opinions, are included in this chapter.

The first questionnaire sent to this new group was identical to the one used in the original research (see appendix A). To avoid influencing the answers in any way, the questions were phrased so that participants would feel no pressure to give any particular answer. The Delphi method is structured to assist "experts" in eventually reaching a consensus without any peer pressure. Findings from the first questionnaires are compared with the second research in the paragraphs below.

Feasibility Study

As previously presented in chapter 5, the initial phase results were as shown below. These are listed in order of the importance attached to their inclusion, as ranked by the participants for the first survey.

Economic Feasibility   83%

Management Involvement   60%

Statement of Objectives   30%

Study of Present System   47%

Additional items included by some of the participants were "User Involvement" and "Planning for the Long Range."

The 1985 Delphi study had some similar items. Matching Economic Feasibility were:

Need for System

Assess Indirect Cost

Tangible/Intangible Benefits

Preliminary Cost/Benefit Analysis

Effects on Profitability

Opinions given in 1985 differed quite a lot from those in 1975, probably because companies have had much more experience with management information systems development.

None of the participants listed "Statement of Objectives" as a needed part of the Feasibility Study portion. Such an omission could simply have been because a current practice in most efficient businesses is goal-oriented planning. Since goals call for a statement of objectives, it is possible that the current participants considered a statement of objectives to be assumed as a part of any feasibility study.

No mention was made of either "Studying the Present System," or "Planning for the Long Range." However, "User Involvement" was listed as a new important requirement of the feasibility study. One of the participants listed "Initiation by the User" [manager]. Since the advent of the microcomputers emphasizes consideration of the user, this answer was to be expected when considering current relations between designers and users.

One respondent commented that in every phase documentation was of paramount importance. The same respondent also stated that the "deliverables were most vital." Such comments reflect current emphasis on both user satisfaction and the importance of some concrete, specific evidence of progress delivered to management.

Requirements Analysis

From the original Delphi, the Requirements Analysis phase listed:

>   Study of Present System   90%
>
>   User Involvement   70%
>
>   Study of Information Needs   70%
>
>   Limits to Costs   47%
>
>   Response Time   23%

An additional item from the 1975 survey was "Specify Short-Run and Long-Run Requirements." For this phase, the 1985 replies were much more in agreement with the original. "Study of the Present System" and "User Involvement" were both mentioned by several respondents, as was the "Study of Information Needs." No one mentioned "Limits to Cost," "Response Time," or "Specifying Short-Run and Long-Run Requirements."

New items added by the 1985 participants were: "User Specifications," "Starting with Problems to be Solved," and "The Deliverables." Inclusion of the last three items was not at all surprising, nor were they all that different from past concepts. However, emphasis on the user and on reports to management are all a part of the present trend toward recognition of the user needs and consideration of the user.

System Specifications

One of the 1975 respondents quibbled about whether requirements should come before specifications, but the issue is really one of semantics. In the 1975 response, these items were the major ones listed under System Specifications:

>   Study of Output   76.5%
>
>   Input Specifications   76.5%
>
>   Study of Data Flow   76.5%
>
>   User Involvement   35.3%

Also listed, with a very low percentile, was "Developing Requirements."

Both input and output specifications could be covered under one of the

1985 responses: "Designed in detail to assure 'apples to apples.' " Although the data dictionary was introduced in the 1985 survey findings, none of the respondents specifically discussed a study of data flow. But one of the respondents who simply wrote a letter of his opinions concerning the current state of the art included an entire paragraph discussing the "mess" of current data within organizations. His suggestions about the importance of data are so pertinent and appropriate to current systems life cycle development that they are quoted in their entirety.

> Another significant change has been the realization that there should be a meta-phase—data analysis and data design. Corporate computerized data generally is messy; data files have been built application by application, with a lot of redundancy, contradictions, etc. I'm not sure that many companies have yet decided to clean up the mess, but they do recognize the problem. When the data is well designed, application development can go much faster, I believe. Good information on this is hard to come by, but I think that objective studies will bear out this conclusion.

User involvement was included by the 1985 participants with such comments as "User Effectiveness" and "User Determination of Specifications." Again, as in other phases, the "deliverables" were mentioned. New items of importance added by the 1985 survey were: "Use of Non-Jargon"; "Evaluation of Hardware/Software Vendor Proposals"; and "Refined Cost/Benefit Analysis."

As with previous phases, the 1985 survey put much greater emphasis on the interface between the designer and the user, with the aim of involving the user in all phases of system design. Such a concern was quite different from the many 1975 responses where the user was ignored. Cost consciousness was certainly ever with project managers of systems. Both the hardware/software vendor evaluation and the refined cost/benefit analyses reflect this trend.

One of the respondents discussed the use of "Prototyping" utilizing fourth-generation languages, program generators, data management systems, and iterative development to give users much faster working systems. According to this respondent, these new methods would also develop accurate and complete system specifications, if a "production" version of the system must be built. These new productivity tools were not available in 1975; thus, a marked difference occurred between the two periods' responses.

System Design

Originally, the 1975 survey listed the following items under System Design:

Identifying and Considering Information Needs   100%

User Support   83%

Built-in Control   83%

Data Base   60%

Integrated System   57%

"Tailoring Systems to Individual Users" and "User/System Interfaces with Both Input and Output" were answers from the 1985 survey to match "Identifying and Considering Information Needs." Evidences of recent innovations in system design and current thinking about systems development were given with "Top-Down Development" and "Prototyping." Although "User Support" was not specifically mentioned, the idea of "User/System Interface" could be construed to include the need for user support.

No mention of "built-in control" was included, although control is widely recognized as a problem with current systems. Although data bases were not specifically mentioned, one respondent did discuss "nonduplication," which may only be possible with data bases. "Review of Detailed Design" might be one respondent's way of introducing the "Structured Walk-Through", since that participant also included "Top-Down Development" and "Prototyping."

Coding and Programming

As with the original 1975 survey, many respondents felt that this phase was a "given" in the design process. The 1975 responses for this phase were:

Standardization   86.4%

Team Approach   81.8%

Accompanied by Documentation   77.3%

Modularity   72.7%

Several 1985 participants actually mentioned that they did not consider "Coding and Programming" as a phase of the life cycle. One even commented that coding and programming "should be a part of all phases." "Maintainability, or Ease of Maintenance" could be construed as meaning a standardized method of coding and programming.

The "Team Approach" was mentioned with an up-to-date version, no doubt patterned after Fredrick Brook's "programmer-team concept." "Accompanied by Documentation" was also included, as was the practice of having a "Work Plan." "Modularity" was not specifically mentioned, but "Integration of Program Modules" implied that the programs would be written as modules and then integrated.

New to this phase was the comment that there should be "Minimum User Involvement." In keeping with the remark that the "deliverable was of prime importance in each phase," the actual coding and programming here would be "the deliverables" for this phase.

This phase possibly revealed more uniformity between the two surveys because coding and programming *per se* have not changed that much. Granted, there are such concepts as top-down development, modularity, and structured walk-throughs; but languages for business programming are still very much the same. Surprisingly, none of the respondents mentioned program generators, which can actually create the code from the planned outline.

Testing

The 1975 responses are given below:

> Measurement through Testing   95.5%
>
> Planning for Testing   95.5%
>
> Parallel Testing   90.9%
>
> Modular, Integrative Testing   81.8%
>
> Independently Generated Test Data   72.7%
>
> Top Management Involvement   68.2%

"Planning for Testing" was implied in the response that stated: "Consider All Logical Paths." "Measure through Testing" was inferred in both the comments "Evaluation of Results" and "Performance of Tests." Under the terms of "Data Security and Integrity" might fall the idea of "Independently Generated Test Data." "Pilot Studies and Analysis" probably replace the "Modular, Integrative Testing" and the "Parallel Testing." "Data Analysis and Data Design" were emphasized in the 1985 survey as being a critical prerequisite to the testing phase. Such comments were not listed in the top items in 1975. "Top Management Involvement" was not included as being currently among the primary considerations, although sixty-eight percent of the original participants listed it as very important during the testing phase.

New items included here are again a result of the ten years' experience that companies have gained in developing information systems. Security, integrity, and actual design and analysis of data for systems are all necessary for systems to be successful. Much of the knowledge gained in each of these areas has come through painful experience in situations where systems have either failed or become inadequate or obsolete.

The original Delphi list included Documentation as a separate phase. Such inclusion depicts the thinking of ten years ago in the systems development field. Even in 1975, business was beginning to recognize the importance of documentation but had not quite reached the point where documentation was always required. Nor had they reached the point where modified programs had documentation reflecting those changes.

Included as important under Documentation in the 1975 survey were:

Completeness in Documentation   100%

Documenting Objectives   100%

Documenting Information Flow   100%

Continuous Documentation   95%

Clarity in Documentation   86%

Data Base Documentation   86%

This phase, documentation, resulted in greater agreement between the two time periods than for any of the other phases. Current acceptance of the need for documentation was evidenced by statements such as: "Should Be Included in Every Phase," "Should Exist in Several Levels," and "Clarity and Completeness." Furthermore, both clarity and completeness were again recognized in the 1985 survey when the respondents submitted important concepts such as "Review of Documentation Adequacy" and included comments such as "Should Be Included in Every Phase."

Because the information systems areas of business today continually emphasize the need for documentation, many of the 1985 respondents elaborated on the necessity for documentation in all phases. One participant even went so far as to state that there should be documentation for (1) users, (2) systems analysts, and (3) programmers. In 1975, management information system experience was not advanced enough for participants to realize the need for differentiation in the types of documentation. For that period, if one could obtain any form of documentation, it was felt that this was a successful accomplishment.

Another concept developed because of increased user participation and because of the awareness that has resulted from years of success/failure is the idea that documentation should be written in language that the user can understand. The statement that there should be the use of "non-jargon" exemplifies this changing attitude toward clarity in documentation and toward documentation especially tailored for particular groups.

Implementation

Paramount for the Implementation Phase in the 1975 study were:

> Planning and Control   100%
>
> Evaluation of the System   100%
>
> Parallel Operation   95%
>
> Capacity for Handling Problems   95%
>
> Preparation for Users   95%
>
> Top Management Involvement   77%

Among the duplicated concepts from the 1985 survey were "Preparation of the Users" and "Planning for Implementation through Education of All Participants." "Evaluation of the System" was also listed under the wording: "Review of Initial Performance Period." Neither "Control" nor "Top Management Involvement" was given high priority by the 1985 respondents. "Parallel Operation" was not even mentioned, possibly because such implementation is very difficult and costly when one is changing from a batch to an on-line system.

Implied in the statements that "the deliverable is most vital" and that one should "Rely on Pessimistic Schedules" might be the ideas of "Capacity for Handling Problems" and "Evaluation of the System".

As with the other areas, the new concepts introduced reflect ten years of experience with development of management information systems. Furthermore, they depict newer methods that have evolved since 1975, such as emphasis upon the user, the need for further training prior to cutover, and the difficulty of meeting schedules.

Summary

From these two studies, many similarities and several contrasting ideas have evolved. The similarities have probably resulted from the fact that even in 1975 there were a number of companies and individuals who were perceptive enough to realize facets important or essential to the success of development of systems. Contrasts have arisen because of many factors:

1. Experience with both successful and unsuccessful system development;

2. New technology and new development methods;

3. Advent of the micro, causing greater emphasis upon the user;

4. Growth of the number of users, also partially resulting from the micro and partially resulting from advances in technology;

5. Increasing awareness of the importance of information to the success of a business;

6. The discovery that information is actually a business resource that *can* be managed.

Increasingly, as technology advances and as the "psychology of programming" and the attempt to satisfy the user achieve more importance, the ability to develop better systems will be a priority item in most organizations. Delphi studies are vehicles for increasing awareness of these changes and pointing the ways in which businesses can manage the valuable information resource.

8

BISCUS/FACS: A Case Study

This chapter reports on the application of the material collected in both the actual literature search and the Delphi studies to a large-scale information system in actual operation. Research included both the writings of renowned authors and the current opinions of experts in the MIS field. The management information system of Southwestern Bell Telephone Company (BISCUS/FACS) is examined through an application of criteria obtained from the research.

BISCUS/FACS: Background Information

The management information system under consideration is entitled BISCUS/FACS, which is an acronym for Business Information Systems Customer Services/Facilities Assignment and Control System. The purposes of such a system appear to be: (1) to assign facilities for the exclusive use of a customer; (2) to create and maintain required records for facilities management; and (3) to maintain inventory records for such assignments. An additional benefit seems to be the acquisition of information useful in routine reporting, forecasting, and planning.

Perhaps a description in layman's terms would add to the reader's understanding of the scope and complexity of such a system. In the BISCUS/FACS system as it is now operating, a person in the commercial department takes a customer's order and from that order codes all the different kinds of telephone service which the customer requests. This information is keyed into SORD (Southwestern Order Retrieval and Distribution), a front-end system which passes the request to the BISCUS/FACS system. Then the BISCUS/FACS system takes over and performs a number of operations, such as generating work orders for telephone installers, checking to see if engineering facilities are available, checking the plant facilities available, and assigning the telephone number, unless manual assignment was requested. The BISCUS/FACS system then sends all information back to the SORD system. In addition, the BISCUS/FACS system assigns the engineering work orders and the plant work orders and checks to locate the nearest available cable or nearest available telephone pole for a customer's telephone.

Another service provided by this system is the aging of telephone numbers which have recently been in service. The aging process prevents recently disconnected numbers from being assigned to new customers before some specified period of time elapses. An additional feature deals with the usage requirements of particular customers, with telephone facilities being assigned to users having larger requirements in a manner to facilitate better service.

Because the catalogue of information contained in BISCUS/FACS has enabled the company to assist in the planning of telephone facilities, still another advantage has accrued to the company and the user. Where apartment houses or business office buildings were being planned, this program considered such needs both before and during construction. By forward planning, the engineering department was able to more nearly determine what facilities were needed. Thus, advanced planning for the installation or construction of needed facilities was enhanced.

A partial list of facilities necessary for providing individual telephone service includes

1. Several cable segments with one cable pair in each segment connected in tandem at interconnection points;

2. Cable identification number;

3. The cable pair number within the cable;

4. The interconnection point where the cable pair is connected to the next cable pair;

5. The binding posts, if required, for the connection; and

6. Identification of the main distribution frame for each customer.

The company must maintain an inventory for all assigned and unassigned outside plant facilities. Inside the central office, a similar number of items must be inventoried and assigned for each customer. This example involved only one customer among the thousands who request telephone service. Multiplying the needs of one customer by thousands should give the reader a feel for the intricacies involved and the paperwork required for efficient operation of a telephone company.

As it is currently operating, the BISCUS/FACS system interfaces with the SORD system, the front-end system. Through the SORD system, information relating to a customer is transmitted to the BISCUS/FACS system.

By a code specifying the type of request, BISCUS/FACS identifies the particular kind of requested service from the service order information. After making the facility assignment (or completing whatever action was requested) BISCUS/FACS transmits the assignment section of the service order and the telephone number back to SORD. In case of an error in the original assignment request, BISCUS/FACS sends the request back to the commercial department along with a notification that an error has been made.

BISCUS/FACS has its own network for everything but the service order. This network includes all the maintenance activity that is needed to maintain inventory and complete other maintenance functions. These operations include: (1) assignment of a line or station transfer; (2) reporting the completion of line assignment; and (3) assignments for the central office, for facilities work orders, and for engineering work orders.

Definition of Key Terms

Describing operations of a specific company, such as Southwestern Bell Telephone Company, usually entails definitions of terms used by the industry but foreign to the general public. For this reason, several of the terms used in this analysis have been defined below.

Central Office: The inside switching equipment needed to connect outside facilities to the switching network for provision of local exchange service.

Commercial Department: That department of the telephone company which deals directly with the customer.

Engineering Department: That department of the telephone company which plans for such connecting facilities as cables, poles, etc.

Plant Department: That department of the telephone company which deals with the actual installation and maintenance of the customer's telephone and telephone service.

Outside Plant: That portion of the work of the plant department which must take place outside the central office or wire center.

Wire Center: One or more traffic units which serve the same exchange outside plant facilities.

Phases of Conceptual Design

As listed in chapter 1, the eight phases of conceptual design considered by this research are: (1) Feasibility study; (2) Requirements analysis; (3) System specifications; (4) System design; (5) Coding and programming; (6) Testing; (7) Documentation; and (8) Implementation. Through all eight phases studied, the conceptual design for BISCUS/FACS followed an iterative process. According to the district data systems manager, these eight steps had to be completed, refined, and then executed again for the BISCUS/FACS programs. Then, elements completed in the initial phases were further refined. As several prominent writers have commented, no line marked where one phase ended and the other began. These phases overlapped and were intermeshed in such a way that one had difficulty finding the exact place where any phase moved into the next phase. Such was the experience of the telephone company personnel in the design of BISCUS/FACS.

Feasibility Study

Economic feasibility was, of course, the primary determining factor for BISCUS/FACS. Closely allied with economic feasibility was the time that would be saved—the time that would come from installing a telephone more quickly, from responding more quickly to a customer's request, from making better use of facilities. All these different estimates for improved service and more efficient utilization of men and equipment were highlighted in the BISCUS/FACS feasibility study.

Although economic feasibility was the study group's number one priority, the planners for BISCUS/FACS did recognize the critical need for top management involvement in every phase of the project. Because a commitment had to be made even before the pilot study was begun in the Dallas office of Southwestern Bell Telephone Company, top management involvement preceded the BISCUS/FACS development there. Going back even further in time, because a commitment had to be made for Bell Labs to begin research for the system, top management involvement also preceded the planning at that level.

Particularly enlightening was the minute detail contained in the cost study. Among the cost items considered were conversion costs, cost for system training and conversion force training, preconversion costs, reprogramming for local systems used as interface with BISCUS/FACS, displaced personnel relocation and retraining costs, computer and computer peripherals costs, maintenance costs for these, site costs, computer control center personnel costs, system support force costs, backup energy costs, communications network costs, and miscellaneous overhead expenses such as energy and miscellaneous supplies.

In addition to the thorough coverage of potential costs for implementing BISCUS/FACS, the planning study also included a detailed description of the possible impact on various departments of the telephone company. Again, the detail was exhaustive with a short discussion as to what each department should expect with the implementation of BISCUS/FACS. These effects were listed by department with specific advantages and disadvantages which might probably accrue to the particular department.

Other incremental savings were considered as a part of the feasibility study phase. Among these potential savings were assignment error reduction savings, recovered floor space, recovered outside exchange plant, recovered line equipment, and line and station transfer reductions. Under each of these headings, a concise estimate of the percent anticipated to be recovered or saved was presented, along with the reasoning behind such expectations.

There were a number of additional benefits which could not be quantified. Included among these were more accurate and timely forecasting, reduction in inquiries because BISCUS/FACS has a centralized file, reduction in transfers because of a facilities control plan, potential savings because of reducing orders previously delayed for lack of facilities, better facilities planning and utilization because of availability of timelier and more accurate cable counts, and reduction in the expenses of inputting and converting to electronic switching systems.

In discussing these anticipated savings with the General Plant Manager (GPM) of the Dallas area for Southwestern Bell Telephone Company, it was learned that the GPM discovered many of the benefits were difficult to measure quantitatively. Among these was the value of improved telephone service, a factor difficult to price. The GPM further stated that, although the benefits from this system were naturally immeasurable both in 1976 and in the immediate future, they could be compared with the implementation of electronic switching systems (ESS). It was evident in 1976 that had ESS not been installed there would not be enough young people in the United States to handle the millions of telephone calls made hourly.

This comparison also should be made in the light of the anticipated growth of communications systems in the United States. Communications systems are not just transmitting voices, they are also transmitting data at very high speeds, especially when transmitting from computer to computer. In view of the country's growing communication needs, the development of the BISCUS/FACS has been of benefit from a research point of view. A viable BISCUS/FACS system is also a benefit to the general public as well. As with so many innovations and inventions, the results of the BISCUS/

FACS research and implementation should yield advantages from which the public in general will profit. Specifically, this system should make telephone service in the future more efficient and more effective.

A study of what Bell Labs and Southwestern Bell Telephone Company did in the area of feasibility of the BISCUS/FACS system revealed that they placed economic feasibility at the top of their list. Naturally, such a study included both technical feasibility and operational feasibility. Since BISCUS/FACS could not be implemented without appropriate hardware and software, a critical factor was the current availability of such computer equipment. Fortunately, the state of the art had advanced so that a data base as large as that required by BISCUS/FACS was feasible. UNIVAC supplied the hardware and actually modified the existing data management system to accommodate the uniqueness of the BISCUS/FACS data base. Since the pilot study began, UNIVAC has updated its hardware. In 1976, the UNIVAC 1110 replaced the 1108 as the supporting hardware. Both the availability of computer hardware and the data management system contributed to the decision to continue with the BISCUS/FACS pilot study.

Requirements Analysis

One factor pertinent to the requirements analysis phase was a list of the objectives for the operating business. In conjunction with this requirement, a company also needed to enumerate the information necessary for meeting the defined objectives. BISCUS/FACS system requirements and objectives were separated into five parts: inventory and assignment objectives, transaction processing objectives, reliability objectives, security requirements, and interface requirements. Each category was then discussed in detail regarding its objective, as well as the requirements necessary to meet the stated objective.

In the earlier phases of BISCUS/FACS development, a Bell System task force compiled a group of objectives for the system. Included in the study group were the Bell Labs personnel, and representatives from both American Telephone and Telegraph and Southwestern Bell Telephone Company. As soon as Dallas was selected as the location for the trial installation, objectives for BISCUS/FACS were integrated into the Southwestern Bell Telephone Company requirements.

One of the primary categories listed above, inventory and assignment objectives, was further divided into: outside plant facility requirements, central office facility requirements, telephone number requirements, requirements for left-in equipment, and requirements for tables such as the Universal Service Order Codes. As each of the subdivisions was included, information requirements for each group were detailed.

Because most readers would be familiar with the concept of utilizing telephone numbers, a partial description of the BISCUS/FACS system objectives dealing with telephone numbers is presented. BISCUS/FACS had as its objective the maintaining of an inventory of all assigned and unassigned telephone numbers for a particular area. From this inventory, the BISCUS/FACS system would assign a telephone number to a service order. In addition, numbers no longer in use would be aged to minimize reuse of numbers listed in the directory. A further objective was to keep up with the number of available telephone numbers through some system of monitoring so that the appropriate people could be notified when this number reached a critical level.

Accompanying the discussion of the transaction processing objectives was a breakdown for the particular kinds of transactions to be processed. These included service orders, central office work orders, engineering work orders, facility work orders, and a section on the requirements for transaction response times. Under the discussion of transaction response times, performance objectives were chosen for the maximum time allowed for the BISCUS/FACS Computer Subsystem to acknowledge the receipt of an input transaction and make the transaction available to the communications system. Included in the objectives were both the time for the system to acknowledge receipt of a transaction request and the response time. Response times were further divided into nominal response times and emergency response times. Objectives were proposed for various categories from within minutes to overnight.

Reliability objectives as they had been established for the BISCUS/FACS system were next listed. These included the number of hours per day the computer system was expected to operate, the number of hours per day in real-time mode, and the objectives for the upper limits to the time the computer was down. Also discussed in detail were the methods for orderly continuation of operations in the event of a computer system outage.

Particularly interesting were the provisions for handling major outages in case of possible computer downtime. These included automatic recovery from audit trails for transactions that were active at the time of the outage.

Other vital factors of the system requirements were both the security requirements and the interface requirements. Security checks needed to meet system objectives were outlined in detail, along with methods for handling security violations. A required security authorization code was also discussed, with provisions necessary for its utilization. Requirements for interface with other mechanized systems of the telephone company were detailed. Since BISCUS/FACS interfaces with SORD and SORD interfaces with the other systems, consideration was given to the impact on these other systems. In the case of Southwestern Bell, the front-end system is the SORD system, which interfaces with both the Customer Records and Billing system and the directory system.

Authors in our study who wrote about "system requirements" agreed that objectives of a system should be transformed into a set of operational requirements. BISCUS/FACS system requirements met this test; detailed operational requirements were listed for all the objectives mentioned. Such items as response time, required reliability, and notification of conditions requiring attention were just a few of the operational details covered.

Study of the present system headed the list of factors thought to be essential for the systems requirements phase of conceptual design. Evidently such a study had been made by the combined task force before the BISCUS/FACS operational requirements were specified. Because every phase of BISCUS/FACS involved required operations to meet customer needs, user involvement was high on the BISCUS/FACS priority list. Furthermore, the BISCUS/FACS system minutely detailed requirements necessary to meet all the stated objectives.

Always paramount in the list of BISCUS/FACS system objectives was the limit to costs. Response time was certainly an essential consideration because one of the foremost purposes of BISCUS/FACS was to speed up the entire service order operation. System flexibility was assured through provisions for emergency situations and considerations of requirements for meeting these emergencies. Overall, the BISCUS/FACS system included the major categories about which the thirty authors in our study wrote when discussing the system requirements phase.

System Specifications

As identified by authorities in the MIS field, this phase should discuss particular specifications a management information system must meet in fulfilling the system requirements. The BISCUS/FACS study included many of the system specifications as a part of the testing documentation. In fact, one entire publication dealt primarily with specifications for testing software. These particular specifications were to determine whether or not the software provided by UNIVAC met the system requirements previously defined.

An amazing aspect of this publication of test specifications was the thoroughness with which the documentation had been accomplished. One of the technical writers commented that perhaps the specifications were too detailed. In answer to an inquiry as to an interpretation of his statement, he remarked that running all of the listed tests had taken so long that probably all of them were not necessary. At any rate, the BISCUS/FACS specifications were very thorough and quite detailed.

Authorities in the MIS field proposed that necessary requirements for viable system specifications should include a study of output, input specifications, and a study of data flow. BISCUS/FACS met the requirements for all three of these factors. The system included a detailed enumeration of outputs required, with specifications necessary for each. The BISCUS/FACS listings even went so far as to give detailed examples of what the outputs should include. Input specifications were likewise minutely detailed by the BISCUS/FACS system, as were the data flows through the system and its interfacing subsystems. As previously mentioned, user involvement was a continual factor in all the phases of BISCUS/FACS design. Developing of requirements naturally were included because these were the actual requirements for which system specifications were outlined.

System Design

For the BISCUS/FACS system, the task force made a very intricate and intensive study of the overall design. Then, this group worked out many of the details of the design at Bell Labs before the trial development was begun in Dallas. Further refinements or improvements to this system are being developed as implementation progresses.

Because transactions are the heart of the BISCUS/FACS system, one category of the system design concerned just the transactions. These were subdivided into the principal types of transactions. Under the overall transaction category, subheads discussed were service order processing, plant and traffic engineering tasks, support transactions, and selected assignment procedures. For each of these subdivisions, details were outlined for items to be included.

Since BISCUS/FACS did not operate in a vacuum, the system design necessarily needed to include subsystems. Both subsystems feeding information into BISCUS/FACS and those receiving processed information from BISCUS/FACS had to be considered. These detailed subsystems were studied and their necessary requirements delineated. Included with the computer subsystem study were the detailed requirements for the operating system, the application programs, and the data base.

An especially intriguing facet of BISCUS/FACS system design was the plan for "rollback and recovery." On-line data bases have caused much consternation because they are susceptible to being deleted either through human or machine errors. To prevent such tragedies, the BISCUS/FACS design team included an audit trail in their system. A record was kept on tape for all operations with an option for an actual paper copy when necessary. Thus, the system contained a history of each transaction entered into the system.

Another intrinsic part of the BISCUS/FACS system was its ability to provide both a "forward" and a "backward" look at previous activity on the system, which was all included in the audit trail. This provision in the system design enabled the user to view the data base as it had been before an operation was executed, and then to look at the data base following the operation. In case of a failure of the system, the user had the ability to "rollback" to the previous point in time or to update the data base with the effects of the transaction through the use of the audit trail. Thus the audit trail provided a method for recovery from failure, human or mechanical, that might wipe out the data base.

The MIS authorities quoted in chapter 4 gave top priority to identifying and considering information needs during the systems design phase. Certainly, the BISCUS/FACS system included this facet in its required factors. Next in importance among criteria listed by the writers were both user support and built-in control, with these two factors being given equal weight. The audit trail and provisions for recovery from failures were excellent examples of built-in control that the designers of BISCUS/FACS included in their plan. User support was previously discussed in detail under the other phases of conceptual design. Such comments were applicable to all of the additional phases as well. The remaining factors identified from the literature, data bases and integrated systems, were integral parts of the BISCUS/FACS design. The entire system was built around a data base, while integrated systems were essential components of the entire operation. The BISCUS/FACS system, then, met the necessary criteria for the system design phase.

Coding and Programming

For the BISCUS/FACS system, the actual data base was handled by a UNIVAC data base language, Data Management System (DMS). Languages for handling the intricacies of a data base and its interface with application programs presented a difficult problem in the initial planning for BISCUS/FACS. A contributing factor in the solution of the problem was the modification of UNIVAC's data base language, DMS. The dominant language used by the applications group to utilize information in the data base was COBOL.

An important factor listed under coding and programming by the thirty authors in our study was the need for standardization. The BISCUS/ FACS system met this vital need by providing that a control committee be consulted to assure standardization. Major areas of concern were system capabilities and their priorities, and interfaces with other elements of the telephone company environment. In addition, the Universal Standard

Order Procedures for writing service orders were followed. Further evidence of standardization came from the feasibility study.

Listed second among the essential factors to be included in the coding and programming phase for a viable management information system was the need for a team approach. From its inception, the BISCUS/FACS system was designed by the team approach method. Even in the beginning, there was joint planning between the parent company, AT&T; its research arm, the Bell Labs; and the trial operating company, Southwestern Bell Telephone Company. Lines of responsibility for various parts of the programming were carefully delineated during the planning phase. Then, these demarcations were followed during the development of BISCUS/FACS.

Probably the highest mark should be given to BISCUS/FACS for documentation to accompany the coding and programming, the third factor highlighted by our thirty authors. In the BISCUS/FACS system, the documentation to accompany this phase was comprehensive. Not only did the planning phase call for every conceivable phase of documentation, but such documentation was actually carried out during the development of BISCUS/FACS. Both graphic and detailed written documentation added to the clarity of coding and programming for BISCUS/FACS.

The final factor recognized by our thirty authorities was the need for modularity in coding and programming. BISCUS/FACS certainly met this requirement. Because the system itself was so complex, the initially planned implementation was scaled down. Further evidence of modularity was apparent by the division of responsibilities. As these responsibilities were outlined, the UNIVAC company was to be responsible for software for the data base manipulation and the operating system software, in addition to hardware. For the BISCUS/FACS programs, input and output were to come from the SORD system and the user department responsible for the inventory of facilities. In addition, the entire BISCUS/FACS system was to be designed and developed for interface with other operating systems of the telephone company. This was to be accomplished by using a standard service order which can be read by all systems.

BISCUS/FACS adequately covered all four of the categories mentioned as being of paramount importance by the writers. In fact, a study of BISCUS/FACS documentation and discussion of the system with involved employees revealed that the BISCUS/FACS system more than met the criteria essential in the coding and programming phase of conceptual design.

Testing

Listed first among the necessary factors for the testing phase was measurement through testing. Following this factor was planning for testing. In both of these categories, the BISCUS/FACS program also excelled. For the planning stage, innumerable tests were designed for the BISCUS/FACS system. Then these tests were actually implemented to measure the viability of the BISCUS/FACS design.

One aspect of BISCUS/FACS found to be particularly remarkable was the depth and intensity of the testing. Among the ramifications of the BISCUS/FACS system tested were the operating system, the data base, the input system, the error codes, and each individual transaction as it traveled through the BISCUS/FACS system. Such intensity in testing indicated that the BISCUS/FACS program met the measurement-through-testing criterion. Furthermore, the comprehensiveness of the BISCUS/FACS testing was evidence of the fact that the testing was modular and integrative. This particular characteristic was the fourth one required by the thirty authors in our study for effective testing of a management information system.

Parallel testing was the third category discussed by these authors. BISCUS/FACS also met that need, since the telephone operation must necessarily be an on-going one. Such a business as the telephone operation could not have information transferred from a manual to a mechanized program without parallel testing.

In meeting the requirement for "independently generated test data," the BISCUS/FACS system went even further and tested using "live" data, with all of its accompanying problems. Of course, data were generated by the programmers as they tested the individual programs. In addition, data had been generated from actual operations and from independent sources during the myriad tests of the system.

Top management involvement was the final category emphasized by our thirty writers for this phase. During the entire testing phase, top management personnel were inextricably involved. They were aware of the inherent problems which could result from errors in such a system and encouraged testing in detail. In addition, they were constantly apprised of the results of such tests, whether the results were favorable or unfavorable.

In this category also, because of the thoroughness of the testing and because the concept of testing was planned from the beginning, the BISCUS/FACS system ranked high.

Documentation

Although the BISCUS/FACS system was impressive for the previously discussed phases, the documentation phase was where BISCUS/FACS should be given a "superior" rating. Seemingly every conceivable aspect of the system was documented. Not only did the developers document before any work was begun, but they also documented at each stage as the work progressed and after completion of the developmental stage.

According to the authors consulted, documentation is so critical that it "makes or breaks" a system. Since the Bell Labs were innovators with the first computer, one should not be surprised that they have evidently realized how indispensable good documentation has become. The entire BISCUS/FACS testing programs and design development were comprehensively documented. There was such detail, such clarity, and such readability in the documentation that even a person unfamiliar with the company operations could easily understand what BISCUS/FACS was designed to accomplish.

Completeness was the paramount concern of our thirty authors under the documentation phase. BISCUS/FACS documentation was divided into two principal groups: deliverable documentation and development documentation. These two divisions were further broken down into detailed parts.

Further evidence of the completeness of the documentation was the documentation for one specific test. For each of the numerous tests run, the documentation included: (1) the purpose of the test; (2) test parameters such as test time, personnel required, and test flow; (3) test inputs along with the input messages described in detail; (4) test outputs along with the output device and possible detailed output messages; (5) acceptance criteria delineating what should happen if the test were successful or the expected results should the test not be successful.

BISCUS/FACS documentation also encompassed the other facets listed by the thirty authors under the documentation phase. Objectives of the system were documented, information flow was documented by both written and graphic methods, documentation was both continuous and clear; and the data base was thoroughly documented.

As previously mentioned, BISCUS/FACS surely was outstanding in the documentation phase. Although "completeness" as a factor probably included all of these other facets, every one of the necessary criterion was met by the BISCUS/FACS system.

Implementation

Number one on our authors' list of factors to be included in implementation was "planning and control," with "evaluation of the system" following second. Actually, one hundred percent of the authors listed both these facets as necessary ones for a viable management information system. BISCUS/FACS was planned and controlled from its inception. Furthermore, the system was constantly evaluated, both in modules and as an integrated system.

Other characteristics considered essential by the thirty writers were parallel operation, capability for handling problems, preparation for users, and top management involvement. In all of these categories, the BISCUS/FACS system rates a "plus." Especially interesting was the preparation for users. Even though the Bell System and Southwestern Bell Telephone Company were among the first users of computers, they still have encountered "people problems" just as other users have. To overcome such difficulties, both the Bell System and Southwestern Bell Telephone Company have concentrated on educating employees who used the computer. In fact, these people have been sent to computer schools, where even the higher levels of management actually wrote computer programs. By participating in the writing of actual computer programs, these executives gained an in-depth understanding of the intricacies of computer programming. They further learned how easy it was to have errors in a computer program and how difficult it was to conceive all the possible permutations for a particular problem.

A particularly impressive aspect of the implementation phase resulted from a discussion with the General Plant Manager of the Dallas area of Southwestern Bell Telephone Company. In the course of a conversation, he revealed that he realized that the current data his company was using had to be "cleaned up" before it could be used with the BISCUS/FACS system. Many top executives from similar organizations had not realized that data useful for manual operations must be revised in some manner for similar mechanized operations. Not only did the Dallas GPM understand the problems involved with the data, but he was also cognizant of difficulties of conversion and expressed an appreciation of the planning which had been accomplished prior to implementation.

The actual operation in Dallas involved building-up a data base by "freezing" the current data at some period in time. This "frozen" data became the base, to which was added any data occurring after the freeze. The data base had to be updated before any live cut-over was actually implemented. Implementation then was achieved with everyone involved working to remove as many "bugs" (errors) as possible before the actual "live" operation. Meanwhile, parallel operations were in progress, so that the BISCUS/FACS portion was simply a back-up to the previous methods. When the system was felt to be operable, then the actual "live" cut-over was implemented.

BISCUS/FACS included all of the factors essential for the implementation phase. The system was planned, controlled, and evaluated. Parallel operation was carried out and the system was designed to handle problems. Users were prepared before, during, and after the design of the system; and top management was involved in all of the phases. As with all of the other phases, the BISCUS/FACS system included the necessary factors for the implementation phase. This system could be used as a model for designing an effective and efficient management information system.

Summary Analysis of BISCUS/FACS

To show the pattern of improvement for the BISCUS/FACS system, the difference in one year of development should be highlighted. In July 1975, a superficial discussion of this system with Southwestern Bell Telephone employees revealed that one of the wire centers was being converted to "live" operation. Since that time, the "bugs" have been worked out of the programs and the whole system has been tested both modularly and integratively. By July 1976, two more wire centers had been added to the BISCUS/FACS system. By September 1976, five wire centers were on the system. This enabled the company to see the effect of having multiple wire centers under the BISCUS/FACS system.

Dallas had additional wire centers to be added to the BISCUS/FACS system on a scheduled basis. Eventually, all the wire centers in the Dallas area were to be placed on the BISCUS/FACS system. Tentative plans as of September 1976 were for BISCUS/FACS to be turned over to the Southwestern Bell Telephone Company as a viable, operating system during 1977.

Interestingly, the BISCUS/FACS developers set the criteria before the programs were written and tested. There were no "after-the-fact" elements, so that BISCUS/FACS was a conceptually designed information system. In fact, this system is said to be the largest business information system in the world to date. The ideas of this system were documented, planned, and then implemented, with a great deal of repetition and iteration in all of these phases.

BISCUS/FACS was designed utilizing the systems approach. The overall system was considered first, then broken down into details, and finally integrated to make a synthesis of the system again. These designers have followed all of the essential requirements listed by experts as being necessary for a workable information system. The enormous size and complexity of BISCUS/FACS make even more remarkable the fact that the system was designed so well. Perhaps, though, the excellence of its design and planning prior to design were really the forces behind its becoming operable.

As an exciting and innovative system, BISCUS/FACS should revolutionize or at least advance applications of management information systems. This trial prepared the groundwork for future management information systems, not just for the telephone company and not just for the communication industry. The untrod territory which the telephone company covered markedly advanced the MIS field and thus was a pioneering effort from which everyone should profit.

1985 Update

Statements in the preceding section were made in 1976, before the BISCUS/FACS system was in complete operation. At that time, the pilot study had worked on one wire center's data and four more wire centers had been added to the system. Since the Dallas area where the pilot study was being run included over seventy wire centers, data from each of these centers was, in turn, added to the system. Although the concept of both customer service and facility assignment was a feasible one, response time from the BISCUS/FACS system gradually slowed as each new center was added. Even with a workable system, computer equipment in 1976 was just not fast enough to yield a viable response time. The net result was that this very large, integrated system had to be broken down into parts. Some of the system was shifted to a minicomputer rather than all of it being processed on the same mainframe. Parts of the system were temporarily abandoned, to be taken up again when computers became faster and more cost-effective. Overall, the design result was an excellent one, but the "state-of-the-art" was just not ready for such intensive integration of data. Timely delivery of information both for installation of the customer's telephone and for information to the service department were of paramount importance. A computerized system that soon became no faster than the previous manual methods was indeed a bottleneck.

According to some of the people currently working in the systems portion of Southwestern Bell, the entire project has not been cancelled. The BISCUS/FACS idea was a viable one, but the immense amount of data to be utilized simply made the computers of 1976 too slow. Current plans are to gradually implement selected portions of the program and eventually achieve the initial goals of the program.

Divestiture and the Bell System

The initial BISCUS/FACS program was a "pilot" program with Bell Labs financing the major portion of the development work. Under the arrangement with AT&T and Bell Labs, before divestiture any one of the Bell operating companies could contract to work on a particular computer project. The original planning was done at Bell Labs; but the project itself was carried on within the local operating company. AT&T funded the major portion of the research with the understanding that the project's results would then be available to any one of the other operating companies. Under such a contract, the BISCUS/FACS programs were developed in Dallas. Not until the pilot programs actually worked did Southwestern Bell assume the complete cost of operation. Such an agreement was a viable means of encouraging participation by the individual companies, who did not feel that they could afford such large undertakings alone.

After divestiture, funding by AT&T was no longer available. Research at Bell Labs and the assistance of their engineers was a thing of the past. The seven operating companies formed out of the Bell network did create their own research facility, called Bellcore, and the arrangement is much the same. However, this organization has neither the personnel nor the years of experience which Bell Labs possesses.

So highly computerized are all of the Bell operating companies that research in more efficient ways of developing, maintaining, and creating management information systems is sure to continue. Not only will these companies be improving and creating new systems for their own operations, but some of them will actually offer software to other users.

Broken Bell

Under divestiture, the long-distance telephone service was awarded to the parent company, AT&T. Local telephone service was separated from AT&T with each of the twenty-two Bell operating companies being incorporated into one of seven regional holding companies. On January 1, 1984, the division became final with the seven holding companies creating an entity similar to Bell Labs. They were each to have one-seventh interest in Bell Communications Research (Bellcore), which supplies technical assistance for network planning, engineering, and software development as well as coordinating the efforts for national emergencies and natural disasters.

Such a move made AT&T a direct competitor with its former operating companies in the area of software and supplies. During the first four months of 1984, AT&T was the leading software advertiser in business publications, according to market researcher C-Systems of Ridgefield, Connecticut. However, AT&T still has a long way to go as a marketing entity, since it will be difficult to change such a large company from a service company to a selling company in a short period of time.

Where does Bell Labs fit into such a scheme? For nearly six decades, Bell Telephone Laboratories have been at the frontiers of research, producing such innovations as the transistor, the bubble memory, and the artificial larynx. With a major part of its budget coming from the system of operating companies, questions arise as to whether "pure" research can now be afforded.

According to George Bylinsky [36:90], "The new AT&T has far fewer resources to underwrite research and development . . . [yet] the party line at both AT&T and Bell Labs is that nothing much will happen over the long run to curtail the Labs' budget." On the positive side, Bell Labs will no longer be restricted from developing products that might make money in the larger marketplace. Under the new arrangements, Bell Labs will no longer be restricted by the Consent Decree of 1956 to license its patents at a reasonable fee. Although there is a slight limitation for the first year, when the Labs will have to provide regional operating companies with any technical information they think will be useful, unlimited licensing has ended.

In the shift of divestiture, people at the Labs are already thinking about how their work can contribute to the bottom line. As Bylinsky states, "more than any other research institution in the world, Bell Labs excels at turning scientific investigation into products" [36:91]. From such research, advances in analyzing, designing, and developing management information systems are sure to follow programs such as BISCUS/FACS. Under the current joint agreement, ways to refine the old BISCUS/FACS program and make it more adaptable to current software and hardware are certainly possible.

9

SABRE: A Case Study

Introduction

The original research for this book proposed the development, from the available literature, of a list of criteria essential to the conceptual design of a large-scale management information system. The "reasonableness" of such criteria was then determined through questioning experts in the management information systems field via a Delphi study. Initially, the idea was that these pertinent characteristics of conceptual design should be helpful to anyone wishing to develop or improve a management information system.

Chapter 8 discussed the application of these criteria as determined from the literature and the Delphi study to the BISCUS/FACS system of Southwestern Bell Telephone Company. This chapter applies the same guidelines to another highly successful company, American Airlines. Just as the BISCUS/FACS system was examined in light of these pertinent criteria, a similar application will now be utilized to examine the American Airlines SABRE System.

American Airlines SABRE System: Background Information

The American Airlines SABRE System was designed and implemented at a time when very few companies were attempting such innovative applications for computers. Because American Airlines was a pioneer in the management information systems field, the original SABRE system was an even more remarkable achievement.

Originally, the title of this system was spelled SABER, an acronym for Semi-Automatic Business Environment Research. Early in the 1960s, the need for a real-time passenger airline reservation system became critical to most airlines. The difference between operating losses and significant profits resulted from a few percentage points in the seat occupancy rate, or load factor. In addition, the federal government ruled that customers materially inconvenienced because of overbooking had to be reimbursed. The SABRE system, then, was designed as a result of economic necessity.

Many books discussing management information systems have given the American Airlines SABRE system as *the* example of a real-time system. Conversely, a number of authors have criticized the categorization of SABRE as a management information system, contending that SABRE was merely a special purpose operational system used to facilitate reservations.

In a personal interview held at Tulsa, Oklahoma in August 1976, Max Hopper, Director of the Tulsa Management Information and Computer Center for American Airlines, responded to this contention by commenting that people making such a statement really did not know about the "back-end" of the SABRE system. Obviously, their knowledge of the intricacies of SABRE was limited to the fact that SABRE was primarily a reservation system. Yet, according to Hopper, SABRE was much more. As documented in the American Airlines Intercompany Manual [5], the original SABRE feasibility study was a plan for a management information system, as well as a reservation system. The outline of this original study revealed that SABRE's purpose included the acquisition of information for management decision.

One of the advantages originally listed for the proposed SABRE system was to have an inventory of seats. In addition, information was to be made available concerning the flight crews, the maintenance operations, and financial and accounting information. Reservations were the paramount concern for the real-time system, but reports for top and middle management were all part of the initial agenda for designing and evaluating the SABRE system. In fact, these myriad management information needs were part of the definition of the American Airlines problem, as well as part of the original feasibility study for SABRE.

Chronologically, the original SABRE system was conceived and designed very early in the evolution of computer systems. A quote from the American Airlines intercompany document, *Introduction to SABRE, 1963*, describes this initial effort.

> American Airlines system is a centralized computer controlled real-time system. Initially its main purpose is to handle reservations.
>
> SABRE presents an evolutionary step in the reservation field, rather than a revolutionary step. Then, the basic idea for doing this is a very simple one: make sure that no passenger record is incorrect or cancelled. [5]

This system was designed when the concept of a management information system itself was very young, undeveloped, and untried. In this time period, even operation systems for computers were in the development stage, hardware was very expensive, and it was not considered feasible to handle large data bases. SABRE was developed in a period before computer hardware or software was available to handle sophisticated programs. In addition, the communication networks needed for a real-time system were quite crude, expensive, and unreliable.

When examining the original American Airlines SABRE system, then, one has to consider the system in light of the state of the art at that time. One must also realize that many of the problems which American Airlines encountered were closely related to technological developments of that time period. Yet in 1963, when the SABRE system was originally designed, this system was quite advanced in both technology and applications of the system concept. In addition, American Airlines pioneered in applying many systems concepts to the business world, especially in the area of fast-response systems.

The original SABRE reservation computer was an IBM 7090 installed in Briar Cliff, New York. Software for the system was developed in a joint effort with IBM. In a personal interview held at Tulsa, Oklahoma, in August 1976, the EDP Systems Manager, C. E. Toma, stated that IBM worked closely with American Airlines in order to gain expertise in the reservations field. Then, the knowledge which IBM gained in the airline reservations field enabled them to develop the PARS (Passenger Airline Reservation System) package. This operating system is currently used by most of the major airlines. Toma stated that at the time PARS became available, American Airlines' own improved system was really superior to the PARS package. However, American decided to utilize the PARS system to be compatible with other airlines.

In developing management information systems, SABRE was just the beginning for American Airlines. After the original SABRE system was implemented, the company experienced a tremendous growth in customers. Evidence of this rapid growth was the sixteen percent increase in passengers in 1964. Although the designers felt that the SABRE system would be adequate for ten years, the original configuration was soon too small. In order to meet this growth, an additional IBM 7090 was installed at Briar Cliff. Because the property around the facility was primarily residential and therefore very expensive, further physical expansion in that location was not practical. As the number of passengers for American Airlines increased and their familiarity and experience with management information systems grew, the need for additional facilities also became apparent.

By 1971, further expansion was needed and both improved software and hardware were planned. American decided to upgrade its computer facilities in preparation for a more sophisticated management information system, SABRE II. They then built the current computer center in Tulsa,

Oklahoma, and installed a Collins C System for the communications network. For the real-time system, the hardware was upgraded from the IBM 7090 to the IBM 360/65. However, the original 7090s were still used for the freight billing program. A current list of the numerous types of information available through American Airlines' management information systems reveals the sophistication of SABRE II. This list runs the gamut from flight profitability to catering services control. American Airlines management personnel felt that almost any type of information needed can be captured and made available for management decisions. Such feelings stem from their pioneering efforts and their vast experience with data bases and real-time systems.

In 1976 Max Hopper revealed future plans for management information systems applications for American Airlines. He felt that American's scarce resources, including pilots, crews, stewardesses, and planes had to be handled more efficiently and effectively. At the time, the company was planning programs which would allow pilots to select their flights. Later, they planned to provide similar capacities for crews and stewardesses. In addition, the company was planning to provide services to travel agencies and to give quicker responses to its own customers. Fuel reporting, parts maintenance, faster bills of lading for freight—all of these were in the future plans for American.

The criteria developed from the literature and from the Delphi study will now be used to evaluate the management information systems of American Airlines. As previously mentioned, the eight phases of conceptual design chosen for this research were difficult to delineate. For American Airlines, as for many other successful companies, these phases have been interwoven. The development of SABRE and the other systems was an iterative process, with each of these eight phases repeated over and over until success was achieved. This chapter will now examine how this innovative, pioneering system fits the criteria developed from the literature and from the Delphi study.

Feasibility Study

Economic feasibility was not necessarily the number one priority for system development for American Airlines, although it was always an underlying consideration. Some method to facilitate having planes fly with passenger loads as near capacity as possible had to be devised. In addition, the company needed to find a solution to overbooking. Seats on an airplane are perishable products and time is of the essence in any solution to overbooking. Evidence of the importance of economic feasibility was listed in the original SABRE document [5]. The projected cost of the original system was calculated on a discounted cash flow basis, with the rate of return on the investment shown to be high enough for the development to continue.

The SABRE document listed the proposed advantages of the SABRE system as: (1) Faster adjustment of inventory; (2) Reduction of airline errors; (3) Elimination of questions; (4) Increased speed of reply to customers; (5) Better image of agent and company to the customer; and (6) Reduction of no-shows. The original outline revealed that reservations were an integral part of the feasibility study, but that they were just one of the categories under consideration. Internal documentation of the original problem in the *Introduction to SABRE, 1963*, had these major headings: (1) What leads to the need for real time? (2) Reservations; (3) Flight and crew scheduling; (4) Inventory; (5) Data collection, etc.

The necessity for fast response was given top priority consideration in the original study. Yet American Airlines also recognized the critical need for top management involvement in every phase of the development. Before any project was approved, the top management studied its Application Proposal Request and then decided at each step whether to continue or stop. All along the way, these executives were apprised of the progress, as well as being told of any time or cost slippage.

To back up the design team, consultants from Arthur D. Little were brought in for an independent evaluation of the system development process. They were asked to evaluate these factors: functional capabilities, timing estimates, equipment, dependability, manufacturer's maintenance organization, and equipment cost. From the first, American Airlines executives felt that these independent observers would give them the true picture of the viability of the system. Furthermore, they asked the Arther D. Little consultants to suggest any needed changes, or to validate the system as it was operating.

From the initial feasibility study through actual implementation, the agent user was involved in the entire conceptual design effort. Agents were selected at random to operate the prototype network developed by IBM. Then, as design progressed, they were constantly consulted about needs and requirements of the agent user. They actively participated in the implementation-testing phase, and were asked to "buy off" before any portion of the system was accepted and implemented.

All of the items covered in the criteria were integrated into the feasibility study of the SABRE system and subsequent improvements to the American Airlines management information systems. Both the user and top management were intricately involved in the feasibility study. Details of the current system for making reservations included a study of the current information flow. Initially, the objectives of the program were outlined and long-range plans were made. Thus, even as early as 1963, the American

Airlines SABRE system included all of the important factors studied during their feasibility phase.

Requirements Analysis

The Delphi response indicated that user involvement was the top priority for the requirements analysis phase, while seventy percent of the writers felt user involvement was a vital category. When system requirements were analyzed, American Airlines officials were very careful to involve the user. The company handpicked five functional experts and asked them to detail the functions a reservation system must perform. In their detailed analysis, these users were also requested to include the decision processes which went into the functions.

According to the SABRE manual, these agents were "not to be biased by the programming consideration of the requirements, nor by how the information could be stored" [5]. People in the general office staff who were responsible for the operation of each major function submitted operational descriptions. Then, for the functions with which they were concerned, each person was asked to "sign off" on these descriptions to indicate satisfaction. The "signing off" was to indicate their satisfaction that the necessary functions would be carried out properly by the system developers.

In addition, throughout the entire process of analyzing requirements for the SABRE system, both IBM and American Airlines officials were required to approve each technical document to insure a continued and clear understanding of the system. How this procedure enhanced the system was clearly described in the SABRE manual: "Misunderstandings do develop. We have had these, but due to the thoroughness of the double check and the close liaison they have so far all come to light *before* the amount of effort to remedy them can be excessive" [5].

As previously discussed, both user involvement and a study of the present system comprised a major portion of the work during the requirements analysis phase. Twenty-four different information needs of American Airlines were listed in this original description manual. Just a few of the management-oriented requirements studied were: management and supervisory, central control, fall-back procedures, management reports, flight summary record, passenger mile performance, both daily and monthly agent revenue and equipment utilization [5]. A glance at just the titles of these requirements revealed that SABRE was indeed designed to provide management information as well as reservation accounting.

Again, as with the feasibility study phase, the American Airlines SABRE system included the primary factors outlined by both the writers and the Delphi study. Users were involved; both the current system and information needs were studied; and costs were balanced against response time.

System Specifications

After the bulk of the functional requirements for the SABRE system was prepared, reviewed, and published, the developers undertook preparation of program specifications and data format specifications. These were divided into two phases, as described in the SABRE manual:

1. A clear set of specifications were prepared, reviewed, and published, which we called Preliminary Data Format Specifications. These were to be basically correct but were lacking in detail. Then, these specifications were frozen.

2. The second phase entailed repreparing, reviewing, and publishing all program specifications as final specifications. These were flow charted where a programmer coder could code from a flow chart. [5]

In order to complete the above-described operations, the developers had to study system inputs, outputs, and data flow. All three elements were examined during the requirements phase, and then the specifications to meet these requirements were devised. Just as the user was closely involved with the requirements phase, so was the user an indispensable part of preparing and reviewing the system specifications. Thus, the American Airlines SABRE system covered the important factors for the system specification phase of conceptual design.

System Design

The original SABRE manual listed an "agenda," which was in essence an outline of the development of the SABRE system. The second major caption of this "agenda" was entitled "System Design." Major considerations here were site location and preparation, and architecture. The architecture portion included the actual system design, and listed program descriptions, control programs, standards, and concurrence procedures. Although the original manual gave only a cursory treatment to the design itself, the current systems manager, C. E. Toma, clarified many of the points. Enlarging on the manner in which such design was carried out, Toma remarked that the functional requirements and specifications were studied and then the general design was developed. Then, this overall picture, or general design, was broken down into modules for programming purposes. All these actions were taken according to set standards, with every step being documented according to company standards. In addition, concurrence procedures were detailed for the designer, programmer, developer, and user. Again, the method of "signing off" previously discussed was implemented.

A comparison of American Airlines activities with what experts felt should be accomplished in system design yielded a high correlation. The company did identify and consider information needs. User support was sought even before the design phase, and user concurrence was necessary before any program design was accepted.

Coding and Programming

Before programming was begun, the company issued a programming standards manual for the SABRE programs. Each program was flow-charted in advance, with standard programming conventions being used. Among coding rules listed in the manual were: (1) The programs were to be coded in segments of 250 or less words; (2) Each segment was to be self contained; and (3) Tests were to be utilized for each program segment before the program as a whole was tested. An outline for the Programming Standards Manual revealed the detail and intricacies of planning for programming. Of particular interest were the sections on standard conventions, techniques and routines, control, and program checkout [5]. To give the reader an idea of the immensity of the original SABRE programs, we note that the control program segment required 25,000 statements, the schedule change and management report programs required 400,000 instructions, the special diagnostics segment required 175,000 instructions, and drivers and simulators and testing device required 200,000 instructions.

Standardization was the most vital factor listed in both the literature search and the Delphi study. Since the American Airlines manual enumerated the procedures for standardizing both the programs and the data base, evidently this factor was emphasized in the design of the SABRE system. From the very first, all of the other pertinent factors were considered in the design of SABRE. The team approach was certainly used, as evidenced by the fact that each category or type of problem was assigned to a project manager. His duties involved breaking the project into its various components and then assigning specific coding requirements to individuals of the team. Documentation was provided even before the programs were written, since one of the initial rules was that the function must first be flow-charted and then programmed. Implicit in the team project and an integrated system was the idea that programs were to be written in modules. These segments were to be so developed that they meshed into the whole system as integrated parts. Thus, on all counts, the SABRE system and the embellishments that followed did use all of the guidelines outlined in this research.

Testing

Because the American Airlines SABRE system was an on-line, real-time system, testing presented problems peculiar to such a system. An on-line system needs to be current and correct as possible at all times. Originally, all of the programs were individually tested. These were then tested as a system before the actual conversion to a real-time operation was completed. In the words of the original SABRE manual, the problem and its solution were clearly described:

> Under full operation, testing in the online environment is still required and since it is impossible to duplicate the full hardware for a second real time system, it is necessary to make use of the online system.
>
> This is accomplished by developing a simulator to run in the offline system which makes use of the online storage load for reads. [5]

In other words, the entries that went into the real-time system were used to test the programs in the simulator. The 1963 manual further remarked: "a true acceptance test has not yet been designed. It is not at all clear how such a test can be developed" [5]. This particular statement was evidently the basis for many of the criticisms of the original SABRE system.

Most of the parts of the SABRE system were tested, with a functional checkout of the integrated parts. The developers conducted an extensive functional and day-to-day operational simulation against a number of actual (past-date) reservation transactions of a scheduled day's flights. The 1963 problem in testing was explained in the SABRE manual as follows:

> If a full fledged valid acceptance test could be designed, the day-to-day monitoring could be relaxed somewhat but it is a large job.
>
> Finally, although a total acceptance test is unlikely, it behooves the user to functionally verify the integrated programs. [5]

This 1963 problem has since been resolved by new software, advanced hardware, and improved programming knowledge. One current method of resolving this problem is through the use of an on-line system data base. Actual transactions are read into the data base and also into a back-up computer which is used for testing purposes. Currently, before any of the new embellishments to the SABRE program are accepted, these are tested totally on the back-up computer. Parallel operations are run and then the "go ahead" given if the extensive tests are satisfactory.

C. E. Toma discussed an outline of the freight conversion and cutover plan that was then being tested and soon to be implemented. Not only was the implementation and testing minutely planned, but there was also a day-to-day and hour-by-hour breakdown of exactly what portion was to be tested and the person in charge of the testing. After extensive testing and comparison of the new programs with the old operation, decisions were made to accept the new procedures or to refine them further.

Even with a real-time system, American Airlines met the criteria obtained through this research. They did have parallel testing, with measurement of the system for testing as a necessary part of that procedure. Planning was a vital part of the testing phase, with the system being tested both in modules and integratively. Test data was independently generated; that is, generated by someone other than the programmers. In addition, by using actual input date, the company had even better test data than could be independently generated.

Another characteristic that should be mentioned for the testing phase was the involvement of the functional units in the testing. This factor could be discussed either under planning or under implementation. However, it should be further emphasized for the testing phase since American Airlines required involvement of functional people in the testing. All during the entire conceptual design, operational people were permanently assigned to the design team. As the project neared the testing phase, these people were asked to play an integral part of the actual tests. They were to physically do the testing, view the results, compare them with expected results, and then to state in writing whether or not such results were satisfactory. For American Airlines, this procedure was not a one-time operation. Instead, the procedure was a continuing measure which resulted in the user being intimately involved with the results well in advance of the actual cut-over.

Documentation

The initial evidence of SABRE documentation was the descriptive manual, *Introduction to SABRE, 1963* [5]. This manual outlined the agenda for studying the feasibility of such a system and included a statement listing the necessity for documentation. Listed under the "System Design" category were the following components of documentation: program descriptions, standards, conventions used, documentation, progress and progress evaluation, how to establish and recognize significant milestones, monitoring and controlling established schedules. From all indications, all of these steps were carried out in the design of the SABRE system. What was remarkable was that in 1963, when many of these ideas were novel and untried, they were incorporated in the original SABRE description manual. Another factor contributing to the advanced ideas and success of the SABRE system was IBM's involvement in the system development. Such evidence as the initial documentation truly depicted how advanced the technical staff was and also indicated at least one reason why American Airlines was successful as a pioneer for on-line systems.

Again, the actual process compared favorably with the listed factors of the documentation phase. The original feasibility study did list the objectives and required documentation of the information flow. Furthermore, the original manual explicitly described requirements for continuous documentation and for a standard to facilitate clarity in documentation. The SABRE system was one of the first to utilize a large on-line data base, so that data base documentation was accomplished with the aid of IBM software. In addition, the user and documentation were paramount considerations of even the original SABRE system.

Implementation

From the initial feasibility study, the implementation phase for SABRE was outlined and planned. Included in the "changeover" category, the SABRE manual outline listed transition planning, interim procedures, meshing of records, and initializing the system. Also included under "System Operations" were numerous plans to facilitate smoother implementation. These were: fallback procedures, recovery procedures, operator training, maintenance of programs, education of user, and acceptance tests [5].

A modified PERT method was devised for determining the critical path and assigning cost values during implementation. All involved personnel held weekly meetings in which project managers discussed the overall picture. Then, for the cut-over, the New York flight managers met with the group. Implementation was gradual, with compatibility between the old and the new being developed while they were in concurrent use. Although implementation was gradual, integration of the system was given paramount emphasis during the entire design and implementation phase.

The major factors listed in the literature and the Delphi study were also included in the implementation phase. Conversion was carefully planned, controlled, and evaluated. Parallel operation was initiated, with the users being educated both before and during implementation. The capacity for handling problems was designed into the SABRE system since every program module had fallback and recovery procedures planned well in advance of implementation. Top management was intricately involved and constantly apprised of the progress of implementation. One should feel that the SABRE system not only met all of the necessary requirements for conceptual design of a management information system, but that they may have at least assisted in "writing the book" for such design.

Deregulation: Airlines in Turmoil

Airlines had minimal competition until 1978. A cover story in the October 10, 1983 issue of *Business Week* states: "In the rare cases in which carriers experienced financial problems [before 1978], a beneficent Washington saw to it that the weak carriers were absorbed by stronger ones." However, the Airline Deregulation Act of 1978 ended that protection and "turned the skies into an aerial free-for-all" [3:98].

Turmoil in the industry was evident as fourteen new non-union jet operators entered the field. Further trouble resulted from suicidal fare wars launched by established carriers such as Braniff. Along with these problems, the larger carriers had difficulty in cutting their costs.

SABRE: A Competitive Advantage

Coupled with the problems facing airlines was the problem of market share. American Airlines used its computer efficiency and its noted SABRE system with enhancements to meet the battle for market share head-on. By furnishing terminals into the reservation system to agents of travel bureaus, American made it very easy for these agents to book flights on their airline. Although all flights at a certain time period were listed on the screen of the CRT, American's flights were always at the top of the list. Such service gave American a competitive advantage in booking flights. Braniff even claimed that American had misused this system to cause Braniff's bankruptcy.

A newspaper article from the *Waco Times Herald* (March 25, 1985) discussed Delta Airlines' new computer reservations system as being the "first totally unbiased" system. The article further discussed American Airlines' reservation system by stating: "SABRE has been under fire recently by officials at other airlines who contend the system gives listings of American's flights priority over those of other carriers." In the same article, a spokesman for American Airlines said: "SABRE's many capabilities have gained wide popularity within the travel community since its introduction in 1976, and we have every confidence that this leadership position shall be retained." The tremendous initial cost of SABRE is still paying off by giving American a more efficient and more competitive place in the airline market.

10

Weyerhaeuser: A Case Study

Background

Turning from an airline system to a forestry system, this chapter now examines Weyerhaeuser's management information system. Again, emphasis is on the guidelines developed in chapters 5 and 6. What the literature revealed and what the Delphi study presented will now be applied to Weyerhaeuser's management information system.

Just as American Airlines developed the SABRE system out of economic necessity, so Weyerhaeuser developed its management information system. The timber industry is a fast-changing one that needs to respond quickly to the ups and downs of American economic prosperity. In an attempt for economic survival, Weyerhaeuser was forced to implement some quicker way for transferring management information.

Like American Airlines, Weyerhaeuser was an innovator in management information systems. Similarly, Weyerhaeuser turned to computer applications to help company employees make use of basic raw materials in a more profitable manner. Basically, Weyerhaeuser is a materials-flow company, starting with land, and from that the basic materials flow into a variety of products. How the company used the flow of these raw materials to different products determined how profitable the company was. Decisions had to be made all along the way regarding allocation of raw materials. Such decisions were critical ones that spelled the difference between whether or not the company was profitable. Situations affecting these decisions changed daily, weekly, and monthly. M. D. Robinson, Senior Vice President of Weyerhaeuser's Pulp and Paper Group, succinctly described the importance of management decisions and the risk involved:

It is of critical importance to the company that that response flow through the system to its highest market values in any given year.

This means that the company's management always has before it a fantastic number of options. These involve diversion of raw material into our various converting businesses.

Within each of these businesses there are literally hundreds of further options, dealing with grade, species, product type, product design, and many other variables . . .

Intuition may help guide management through this maze of options, but few of us have that much intuition. On the other hand, rational decisions require good—and rapid—information and a system for its conveyance to the right people at the right times. [159:45]

In a report to the Society for Management Information Systems, C. E. Carpenter, Director of Business Systems for Weyerhaeuser, discussed company progress in the areas of systems and computers. This report candidly discussed the Weyerhaeuser approach, the principles they tried and are trying, and how they "went from a standing start in 1962 to a major effort almost immediately" [141:59]. Carpenter enumerated Weyerhaeuser's achievements in management information systems, but was also frank enough to remark that such progress had not been an "unmitigated success."

Discussing the development of the MIS function within Weyerhaeuser, another company executive, K. V. Abraham, Manager of Operations Research, divided these developments into three phases—Phase I: 1962-1966; Phase II: 1967-1969; and Phase III: 1969-1971 [1]. Since his article describing these phases was written in 1971, Abraham naturally did not describe activities after that date. These same phases were discussed by Carpenter when he described the MIS design of the Weyerhaeuser management information system. Much of Carpenter's presentation will be discussed under the applicable phases of conceptual design. Particularly appropriate here, though, is Carpenter's remark that in 1962 the only data processing at Weyerhaeuser was some accounting applications. Thus computer development at Weyerhaeuser paralleled the history of development of computer utilization historically.

Both Abraham and Carpenter revealed that few of the Weyerhaeuser management people were familiar with systems or data processing in 1962. Yet Carpenter remarkably stated that: "there was the conviction that we had to get involved with computers if we were to be a growth company" [41:59].

Since Weyerhaeuser was an innovator for many MIS concepts, the company's pioneering effort was both slow and costly. In addition, many applications came at a time when neither software nor hardware was advanced enough to handle the planned applications. For one particular application, Weyerhaeuser had to develop its own operation system in partnership with General Electric. As with many such early developments, the project became larger and more complex than originally estimated. In describing the effects of this experiment, Carpenter stated:

This whole episode was a crippling blow to the credibility of systems in Weyerhaeuser because so much of the applications effort was aimed at using the promised hardware/ software capability. Its delays caused delays in achieving the promised results for line management. As a result the systems effort gained a reputation for not delivering, for being enamored with technical aspects of the functions, and for being out of control. [41:60]

Even with the negative aspects of designing the first system, many benefits did accrue and Mr. Carpenter's report also listed these. Among the major benefits were a decrease in processing times for orders from two weeks to two days and reports giving status of orders and the market.

Weyerhaeuser began computer utilization out of economic necessity. In order to become a growth company, they launched a massive system effort in 1962 when the management systems effort was in its infancy. In spite of mistakes generated by over-enthusiastic people and by the unavailability of the necessary hardware and software, the company made giant strides toward achieving its goal. Even with its flaws, the Weyerhaeuser management information system did improve decisions and certainly did make information available on a more timely basis.

Each phase of the design of the Weyerhaeuser system will now be discussed in regard to the actual concepts used and those concepts which experts felt should be used. In many instances, how the original Weyerhaeuser system developed will be contrasted with current practices of the company. These current practices were described in a personal interview with a Weyerhaeuser representative held in Tacoma, Washington in August 1976.

Feasibility Study

In 1963, the original feasibility study was initiated by George Weyerhaeuser, the company president. Its purpose was to determine how systems and computers could be used to improve the management capabilities in the wood products or building materials division of the business. From this study evolved a recommendation to develop an integrated management information system built around entering a basic order for wood products. Economic return on investment was one of the primary considerations behind the recommendation. Although cost data were not available, the Weyerhaeuser representative stated that economic feasibility was one of the major decisions for originally undertaking any new application system.

In the 1972–1975 period of economic decline in the U.S., not only was economic feasibility required for undertaking any new application; according to the company representative, it was almost the *only* criteria for undertaking a system. However, current company management is now willing to undertake programs where economic benefits are not tangible and visible. Recall that both the Delphi participants and the writers ranked economic feasibility high on the list of requirements for the feasibility study phase.

The writers mentioned the need for user involvement, but the Delphi respondents ranked this facet in first place. Evidence of user management and top management involvement appeared in the description of the MIS design at Weyerhaeuser. Reorganization for developing the MIS program at Weyerhaeuser called for the business system branch to become a corporate entity reporting to the president. In line with this change, the decision was made to centralize the major computing efforts of the company, with corporate control of all data processing. These decisions were made in 1966, but are still in effect today.

Management involvement was an early systems management principle implemented by Weyerhaeuser. Early in their system development, Weyerhaeuser recognized that the need for line management involvement was critical to the success of the management information system. According to the report by Carpenter [41:61], line managers were full-time participants in the general feasibility study, which resulted in three- to five-year system plans for each division.

A statement of objectives and a study of the present system were other pertinent factors included in the guidelines for the feasibility study phase. The lucid quote given below from Carpenter's article on system design addresses both of these topics.

> Planning for a full set of systems applications for a business was regarded as mandatory. The objectives were to define priority needs, to have a stable development program, to design common data bases, to have compatible systems, and to provide adequate lead time for hardware/software installation. The primary vehicle for achieving this was the comprehensive feasibility study, which covered all of a division's known system needs and generated a five-year development plan . . . [41:61]

All of the factors listed by the writers and the Delphi experts as being important for the feasibility study were a part of the Weyerhaeuser development of its original information system.

Requirements Analysis

Both top management and user management at Weyerhaeuser were involved in the requirements analysis, as a part of the comprehensive feasibility study. As described previously, the study covered all of a division's known information system needs. Since these managers were explicitly involved in the entire conceptual design, they constantly contributed to the descriptions of the company requirements. Thus, the top three factors for the requirements analysis phase were included in the Weyerhaeuser MIS development: users were involved; the present system was studied; and the information needs of the company were studied. Since five-year development plans were prepared, evidently both short-run and long-run requirements were also specified. Not specifically mentioned were limits to costs, but this feature might be implied from the idea that economic feasibility had top priority.

System Specifications

One of the early system management principles for management involvement at Weyerhaeuser stated that line managers were to be full-time participants through the entire system design. Furthermore, these managers were also to be participants in the detailed specifications of major systems. Originally as well as currently, the user helped define requirements and either participated in developing the requirements or at least reviewed specifications. Thus, in the Weyerhaeuser system development process, the input, output, and data flow were all considered to be part of studying the present system. In addition, the user was inextricably involved in developing requirements and specifying needs.

The Weyerhaeuser executive interviewed stated that the key concept which the company tried to follow was always to identify a client for each application. This client was from the user group primarily responsible to assure that the application met his requirements. Since he was the key decision maker who finally had to "buy off," he had the responsibility for seeing that the specifications were detailed and complete. As this executive remarked, "the alternative was an ad hoc user committee where nobody had responsibility for success or failure of that system."

System Design

At Weyerhaeuser, involving the user called for his identification and consideration of information needs. Both the writers in our study and the Delphi participants gave this factor number one ranking. Under the original system plan at Weyerhaeuser, user support was mandatory since line managers were required to be full-time participants in the entire design development.

The difficulty involved in designing a common data base caused many of the problems in the original Weyerhaeuser programs. Because applications for the various segments of the corporate business were similar, the company envisioned common data bases for such facets as customer files, vendor files, and compatible data structures. Originally, Weyerhaeuser developers planned to have four processors and the data base all linked to a common core. Quoting Carpenter, "The magnitude of the payoff of this concept was recognized and eagerly desired; the magnitude of the risks were grossly underestimated" [41:60].

Where the Weyerhaeuser people ran into problems was with the operating system. Even with the joint effort from both Weyerhaeuser and General Electric, the company did not get fail-soft multiprocessing or the ability to access a common data base from any computer. In discussing the problems encountered and the lessons learned, Carpenter explained, "developing basic operating software is too expensive, too complex, and too risky for corporations that are not in the software business" [41:60].

Even from the beginning, the Weyerhaeuser people planned for integrated systems. In fact, the initial recommendation was for an integrated management information system for the wood products order entries. In discussing problems evolving from attempts to meet this objective, Carpenter remarked, "it is virtually impossible to develop integrated systems under changing objectives and priorities that are not in the framework of a long-term plan" [41:61]. To alleviate this problem, a number of changes were made in the Weyerhaeuser principles guiding the systems effort. Among these was the establishment of a new position of system planner, whose duties were to develop long-range systems plans well related to business requirements.

Possibly of more interest among the guiding principles for the system effort was a general guideline for new systems development. The purpose of this guideline was to make these systems as common, transferable, and modular as possible. As Mr. Carpenter described the principle,

> The objective of commonality is to assure that systems performing a similar function are as common across the division, group, or the company as possible in order to minimize redevelopment and maintenance costs. The transferability objective is to assure equipment independence for systems that are to be processed in the field. The modularity concept is that systems are designed and programmed in modules in order to improve their maintainability and flexibility to meet new requirements. [41:70]

Further in the same paragraph, Carpenter in essence indicated that the programmers had been only giving "lip service" to building modular systems. The Weyerhaeuser representative interviewed reported that the company is currently using the Hoskins concept of modular programming, which is essentially structured programming. This gentleman further commented that he felt most people who said they were integrating systems and designing modular programs were probably not doing so. According to him, structured programming was not the natural way to program, and many programmers tended to be undisciplined. However, Weyerhaeuser did and does try to promote both modular programming and modular system design. Modular system design was defined as a hierarchical approach, while modular programming was defined as a structured approach.

Coding Phase

From the very first establishment of the corporate computer center, Weyerhaeuser has used COBOL and FORTRAN as the standardized programming languages. In standardizing the languages, their stated objectives were to provide a design reference point for systems and to promote transferability of systems. In the mid–1970s seventy percent of the Weyerhaeuser programming was in COBOL, twenty percent was in FORTRAN, and ten percent in other languages. For corporate accounting purposes, Weyerhaeuser is using the MARK IV Informatics data base language. Although the use of MARK IV had not been significant by 1976, the company planned to use MARK IV as a programming language in the future. Since the headquarters' computers are manufactured by Honeywell, the Weyerhaeuser people felt there was a possibility of their using the Honeywell language similar to MARK IV. This Honeywell language has the title MDQS, which is an acronym for "management data query system." Modularity in programming was previously discussed under the system design phase. Since Weyerhaeuser felt that modularity is important, the company was trying to promote both modular programming and modular design.

Standardization in coding was the top factor mentioned by both studies. In answer to a direct question about the company policy toward standardization, the Weyerhaeuser representative remarked that hard and fast standards were minimal and related to the operational areas. Weyerhaeuser does have documentation standards, and standard identification of data names and programs. However, the company does not force management programming standards, except to state that programs should be structured. Their feeling is that structured programming is more a practice than a standard.

For the coding and programming phase, Weyerhaeuser has followed some but not all of the guidelines listed. However, company representatives were quite candid in discussing Weyerhaeuser philosophy about these factors. The company representative reported that standardization and modularity factors advocated by the guidelines were certainly desirable; but at Weyerhaeuser, such guidelines were not always implemented.

Testing Phase

In the Weyerhaeuser organization, the developer was and is responsible for most of the testing. The company has not involved the user directly in the testing. However, the final acceptance testing of the product must be performed by the user, who has been asked to "buy off" for the finished product. In taking the program all the way from the feasibility study through the finished product, the developer has the responsibility to plan and implement all the testing. Because the developer has been primarily responsible for the testing, he must measure through testing. Since the overall Weyerhaeuser plan has been for modular and integrative programs, somewhere in the developmental stage the program module must be integrated into the system. Not until this integration has become a reality has the developer been cleared of responsibility for the project's success.

For the central computer service center, no program has been accepted as a routine, on-going production system unless the program has been tested for quality assurance. Such testing has included determining if the documentation was adequate, if the program met operational standards, and if the program system could be run by the service center. In essence, then, quality assurance has been one of the phases of the testing process.

Weyerhaeuser has not followed the philosophy of having independently generated test data. As previously discussed, the test data generation has been part of the general responsibility of the developer. However, the company did purchase a good test data generator package called Test Master from the Hoskins Company. This package has not been used extensively, according to the report of the Weyerhaeuser representative.

Top management has not been actively involved in the actual testing since the company method has been to have the developer carry the testing through until system completion.

Documentation

Documenting objectives was the one facet of the documentation phase given greatest emphasis by Weyerhaeuser personnel. Throughout their system process, emphasis has been on documenting objectives as much as on documenting the entire system. After these objectives were documented, the user has been asked to review them and then "buy off." Such user acceptance has been done very formally to assure both user involvement and user satisfaction with the system. At each decision point in any system development, the user has reviewed what has been accomplished up to that decision point, and accepted or rejected this work. Then, the user decided whether to continue or stop the development. Both of these decisions have been accomplished very formally so that a written record would be available for future reference.

The Weyerhaeuser representative stated that their documentation was supposed to be complete and continuous. However, he felt that Weyerhaeuser was like anybody else; documentation was not done as early nor as well as it should have been. Since documentation depended on the individuals involved, some documentation was better than others. The data base, though, has been documented.

Implementation

The primary guidelines listed by both the writers in our study and the Delphi participants were a part of the implementation phase at Weyerhaeuser. Not only was implementation planned, it was also controlled. Although the company had no specific evaluation program for the system, the validation by users yielded constant evaluation through use.

Because much of the Weyerhaeuser programming has been for on-line systems, they found parallel implementation often difficult. Yet, the company used parallel implementation as much as possible.

Users were prepared, since they were inextricably involved throughout the whole process. They had to be cognizant of procedures in order to make evaluations at each decision point. Top management was closely involved ever since the decision to move the computer center and the business system function to corporate headquarters. As part of the management involvement and user involvement, the "buying off" procedure assured Weyerhaeuser that their systems had the capacity for handling problems. Thus, under this category as with all of the others, Weyerhaeuser would score high in meeting the guidelines.

Weyerhaeuser Update

A December 2, 1985 *Forbes* article gives the current picture of Weyerhaeuser by stating that "the tree no longer dominates." The article then explained that Weyerhaeuser has had to diversify to survive. Paramount in the diversification has been their strong management information system that enabled them to "channel roughly $500 million annually into pulp and paper manufacturing as a means of better using the company's timber assets." By early entrance into use of a valuable information program, Weyerhaeuser was able to develop "one of the most efficient manufacturing assets in the world." Although, as previously discussed in this chapter, Weyerhaeuser entailed more expense by being the innovator in developing management information systems for its operation, these early expenditures are paying off in a time when the timber industry is very depressed. Once again, a viable management information system has paid off in immeasurable terms.

11

Summary and Conclusions

One of the primary objectives listed for this research was to search for guidelines common to successful management information systems. The feeling was that a study of the literature, the questioning of leading experts, and an examination of three successful systems should define and evaluate factors which are critical in the design and implementation of large-scale management information systems.

As background, this research chronologically traced the development of computer utilization in business. Next, a study was made of published writings in the management information systems field. The purpose of such a study was to search for unanimity in thought as to which factors were important in the conceptual design of a management information system. Among those noted writers in the MIS field, a number of areas of agreement were discovered.

Because there were so many possible research directions, this study had to employ "tunnel vision," ignoring many other areas related to information systems. Such vital issues as security and individual privacy were not explored.

Before listing specific conclusions, this chapter summarizes findings for each of the eight phases of conceptual design. Included in this summary is a comparison of the literature findings and those from the Delphi study. Comparisons and contrasts have been presented in both table and explanatory form.

Feasibility Study Summary

Both groups listed economic feasibility, management involvement, and a study of the present system. Writers ranked economic feasibility first, while the participants of the Delphi study ranked it third. Current opinion seemed to indicate that economic feasibility was important, but that other things were of equal or greater importance for the feasibility study stage.

Listed second by both groups was management involvement. The composite thinking of the authors emphasized the statement of objectives, while the current Delphi respondents used planning for the long range. Semantics might be responsible for the apparent difference, since long-range planning might well include a statement of objectives. The outstanding discovery from the Delphi study was that user involvement and a study of user attitudes and expectations were highlighted. These elements were evidently given more emphasis in current development than they were in earlier stages of the development of management information system conceptual design. Generally accepted ideas or principles for the conceptual design of a management information system were presented from the literature search. Thirty authors who had covered conceptual design of management information systems in depth and who wrote in the period 1966 through 1976 were consulted. Many of these writers were also on the expert Delphi panel.

These were not the only authorities writing about management information systems during that period, but were selected according to specific criteria. The first criterion was that the authorities be well known in the MIS field and that their writings be well accepted. All of the thirty individuals selected for the literature search were recognized as people knowledgeable in the MIS field. An additional criterion was that these authors had discussed the majority of the eight phases of conceptual design being considered.

Previous chapters have discussed the idea that the classification of conceptual design into phases was an arbitrary one. Also mentioned was the concept that none of the particular writers was forced to fit his ideas into this framework. Instead, as the writers were studied, their thinking revealed that the entire conceptual design process was an iterative one. Delineating any particular phase thus presented a particular problem. Writers were, therefore credited for specific concepts or guidelines discussed whether these fit a particular phase or not.

Table 21 depicts the vital interest shown in user attitudes, involvement, and expectations.

One common thread of agreement ran through the two groups. Economic feasibility was important for both, while management involvement was certainly unanimously highlighted. In addition, studying the current system ranked high on both lists. Therefore, commonality of thought did exist under the feasibility study phase.

Requirements Analysis Summary

Both the literature summary and the Delphi study listed all four of the top items under the requirements analysis phase. Slight disagreement was evidenced in the order of importance attached to several items. Studying the

Table 21.   Comparison of Feasibility Study Phase: Literature vs. Delphi.

Factor	% Discussing Factor	Rank for Delphi Round 3
Economic Feasibility	83%	3
Management Involvement	60%	1 (tie)
Statement of Objectives	60%	—
Study of Present System	47%	5
ADDED BY DELPHI STUDY		
User Involvement	—	1
Planning for Long Range	—	4

present system was ranked first for the writers, while the Delphi respondents only awarded this factor third place, as is shown in table 22.

User involvement was first in the Delphi study and second with the writers. Study of information needs was rated second by both groups. In addition, both listed cost constraints as number four, while the authors ranked response time in fifth place. At this point, the unanimity ended, with the Delphi participants emphasizing short-run and long-run requirements while the writers listed system flexibility as one of the categories. Again, though, there was evidently a great deal of agreement about which items should be included as important for the requirements analysis phase.

System Specifications Summary

Although rankings for the individual items by the two groups were quite different, both studies included the same five factors under the systems specifications phase. The writers specified that output, input, and a study of data flow were all of equal importance for the top ranking. On the other hand, the Delphi participants classified output as second, input as fourth, and a study of the data flow as fifth. With only thirty-five percent of the writers discussing user involvement in the specifications phase, this item received a very low rating, yet the Delphi respondents considered user involvement the top category for this phase. Current emphasis on user involvement may be attributable to experience gained by actual practitioners. The importance of user involvement, then, should not be overlooked. As the Weyerhaeuser representative we interviewed remarked: "Some few systems may be successful without user involvement, but almost all successful systems have it." User involvement ranking for the system specifications phase is depicted in table 23.

Table 22.   Comparison of Requirements Analysis Phase:
Literature vs. Delphi.

Factor	% Discussing Factor	Rank for Delphi Round 3
Study of Present System	90%	3
User Involvement	70%	1
Study of Information Needs	70%	2
Limits to Cost	47%	4
Response Time	23%	Included in 4
ADDED BY DELPHI STUDY		
Specify Short-run & Long-run Requirements	—	5

Table 23.   Comparison of System Specifications Phase:
Literature vs. Delphi.

Factor	% Discussing Factor	Rank for Delphi Round 3
Study of Output	77%	2
Input Specifications	77%	4
Study of Data Flow	77%	5
User Involvement	35%	1
Developing Requirements	18%	3
ADDED BY DELPHI STUDY		
File Design	—	4 (authors) only)

The importance of user involvement may be one of the outstanding findings from the Delphi study. As previously mentioned, in four of the eight phases the Delphi participants listed user involvement as the paramount factor.

Although developing requirements was given a very low rating by the authors from the literature search, this factor was listed second by the Delphi authors alone and third for the composite Delphi group. File design was not given the emphasis in the literature that it was given by the Delphi respondents.

System Design Summary

Under actual system design itself, unanimity existed in the top category, as depicted in table 24. With identification and consideration of needs being listed first by both groups, a surprising turn-around was evident regarding user support. In the previous categories, the Delphi participants had ranked user involvement as first for all three phases. However, under the actual system design, the Delphi respondents gave user support only a number five ranking. Possibly the Delphi participants felt that if user support were actually involved in the first phases it would not be so vital in the design phase. In direct contrast, the writers ranked user support higher under this system design phase than they had ranked the factor in the previously discussed phases.

Once more, differences may be attributable to semantic differences or to the arbitrary classification of the entire conceptual design into the eight phases chosen. The respondents may have had difficulty in delineating which factor was more important for a particular phase since each phase ran into the next phase. The pertinent characteristic emphasized for the system design phase was user support.

The literature search covered a much longer time period than the Delphi study. During the time span of our literature review, data bases were not technically possible for part of the period except for companies with a great deal of expertise and money. Even so, data bases were at least mentioned by sixty percent of the writers and were ranked third by the Delphi participants.

Integrated systems were discussed by both groups. The Delphi participants ranked such systems second, while fifty-six percent of the authors considered this factor vital to successful system design. Because integrated systems have become more feasible as technology has advanced, the Delphi participants placed this factor higher on the list then did the writers in the literature searched.

Built-in control was not mentioned in the top five categories of system design by the Delphi group, nor was the design method considered in the top categories by the authors. Again, though, four of the top five factors were common to both studies.

Coding and Programming Summary

Unanimous agreement existed for three of the categories under the coding and programming phase. Standardization was the factor ranked first by both groups; i.e., both groups thought that coding should be standardized. Coding accompanied by documentation was the number three choice for

Table 24.   Comparison of System Design Phase: Literature vs. Delphi.

Factor	% Discussing Factor	Rank for Delphi Round 3
Identifying and Considering Information Needs	100%	1
User Support	83%	4
Built-in Control	83%	—
Data Base	60%	3
Integrated System	57%	2
ADDED BY DELPHI STUDY		
Method of Designing	—	5

both groups, while modularity in coding was second for the Delphi study and mentioned by seventy-three percent of the literature writers, as shown in table 25.

Utilizing the "team approach" to coding and programming was another category listed by the literature, but not by the Delphi respondents. Because any sizeable project would necessarily have to be broken into parts and coded by members of a team, this particular concept may have been "assumed" by the Delphi group.

Of especial importance in this phase were the factors listed by the Delphi participants, but not highlighted in the literature. These factors depicted current thinking about both systems and management information systems and included established goals for programmers, test data development, and integration of code numbers into a total system of codes. For this phase, also, a commonality was evident between the two groups, with the top three factors being covered by both.

Testing Summary

Possibly the greatest degree of agreement came under the testing phase. The first five categories selected by each group were identical, although the individual rankings were somewhat different. Many of the literature rankings were in the upper ninetieth percentile. In comparing rankings with such high percentages, one has difficulty in delineating importance.

Both groups felt that parallel testing was vital. All the Delphi participants, except the business group, ranked this factor first, while the literature group awarded parallel testing a third place rating. Although the authors thought measurement through testing should be first, this item was

Table 25. Comparison of Coding and Programming Phase:
Literature vs. Delphi.

Factor	% Discussing Factor	Rank for Delphi Round 3
Standardization	86%	1
Team Approach	82%	—
Accompanied by Documentation	77%	3
Modularity	73%	2
ADDED BY DELPHI STUDY		
Established Goals for Programmers	—	4
Test Data Development	—	5
Integration of Code Numbers into Total System of Codes	—	5 (businessmen only)

ranked fourth in the final Delphi round. Planning through testing was third in the Delphi study and second in the literature search. Modular and integrative testing were rated second in the Delphi and fourth in the literature search, while independent test data generation was fifth for both groups, as shown in table 26.

A great deal of unanimity also existed under the testing phase. Although some of the Delphi responses did include top management involvement for the testing phase, this factor was not ranked in the top five categories. However, the writers listed the involvement of top management as one of the five most important items for the testing phase.

Documentation Summary

Several pertinent ideas evolved from the responses to the documentation phase. All of the top four categories from the literature search were listed under at least one of the Delphi rankings, as depicted in table 27. Both studies ranked completeness in documentation first. While the writers gave documenting objectives a second place rating, the Delphi respondents listed this factor as number four in the second round and did not rank it in the other rounds. Although documentation of information flow was third from the literature search, the Delphi respondents gave it only a fourth place rating.

Both lists considered continuous documentation important, as well as

Table 26.   Comparison of Testing Phase: Literature vs. Delphi.

Factor	% Discussing Factor	Rank for Delphi Round 3
Measurement through Testing	95%	4
Planning for Testing	95%	3
Parallel Testing	91%	1
Modular, Integrative Testing	82%	2
Independently Generated Test Data	73%	5
Top Management Involvement	68%	—

Table 27.   Comparison of Documentation Phase: Literature vs. Delphi.

Factor	% Discussing Factor	Rank for Delphi Round 3
Completeness in Documentation	100%	1
Documenting Objectives	100%	—
Documenting Information Flow	100%	4
Continuous Documentation	95%	3
Clarity in Documentation	86%	—
Data Base Documentation	86%	5
ADDED BY DELPHI STUDY		
Documentation for User	—	2

data base documentation. Clarity in documentation was the factor omitted from the Delphi study but included in the literature listing. Perhaps the Delphi participants considered this factor of documentation as a part of completeness. The one factor included by the Delphi respondents but not specifically covered by the writers was documentation for the user. As user involvement has grown in importance, so has preparation of the user. Therefore, the increase in emphasis on user involvement could certainly account for the inclusion under documentation for the user.

Implementation Summary

Under implementation, the Delphi respondents mentioned all of the first six items gleaned from the literature search. Percentages for the writers were so high that the variation in importance must be considered to be only a slight difference. User preparation was ranked first in the Delphi study, while ninety-five percent of the writers stated that this item was important in the implementation phase of conceptual design. The writers listed planning and control in first place along with evaluation of the system. In contrast, the Delphi participants ranked planning and control second and did not even list evaluation of the system in the top five for the third round of the Delphi. However, during the second round, the Delphi participants did rank evaluation of the system in third place. Table 28 depicts the contrast in ratings.

In their final Delphi ranking, only the business participants ranked parallel operations in the top five. Capacity for handling problems was given ninety-five percent coverage in the literature search, but was only fifth in the third-round Delphi rankings. Although top management involvement was rated third by the Delphi participants, the literature search yielded only a sixth place. Phased implementation was the only factor mentioned by the Delphi respondents that was not covered by any noticeable percentage of the writers.

Once more, as with all of the previous phases, a high degree of unanimity existed. Both groups agreed on a majority of the categories for the implementation phase, as they did for the other seven phases. Where differences existed, they were in most respects differences of degree and not of content. Perhaps the most remarkable finding from both studies was the number of instances in which both groups agreed on the factors to be included in the phases of conceptual design.

Overall Summary Comparison

Table 29 gives visual evidence of the high degree of commonality which existed between the two studies. An overall comparison of these eight groups and the top categories of both the literature search and the Delphi study shows unanimity in many instances.

In table 29, the factor listed first from the literature search has been given. In another column, for this same factor, the Delphi ranking for that category is given. Then, where the top category for the literature and the Delphi differ, the factor ranked first in the Delphi is also shown.

Under the system design, coding and programming, and documentation phases, both groups gave number one priorities to the same factors. For the other groups, the comparison is given in table 29. In most instances, the factor ranked number one from the literature was in the top five from the Delphi study, but the levels often were different. An outstanding finding was that the Delphi respondents gave user involvement the top ranking for all of the first three categories.

Table 28. Comparison of Implementation Phase: Literature vs. Delphi.

Factor	% Discussing Factor	Rank for Delphi Round 3
Planning and Control	100%	2
Evaluation of the System	100%	—
Parallel Operation	95%	—
Capacity for Handling Problems	95%	5
Preparation for Users	95%	1
Top Management Involvement	77%	3
ADDED BY DELPHI STUDY		
Phased Implementation	—	4

In a similar pattern, the Delphi group gave user preparation first place for the implementation phase. These findings were indicative of the current mood in conceptual design of management information systems. Since the user makes or breaks the system, his importance in the success of a management information system has at last been recognized. Practitioners, writers, and organizations themselves have discovered that additional and continual emphasis on making the user aware of the capabilities of the system is vital to system success. From such discoveries has evolved the idea of consulting the user in advance of the actual system design and continually consulting the user during the other phases.

The only other category where there was any marked difference was under the testing phase. The Delphi study showed parallel testing to be most important and only ranked measurement through testing fourth and planning for testing third. Since the differences here were so fine, they could be considered a matter of scale, or a result of the testing methods. All of these factors were considered important in the conceptual design of a management information system.

Application of the Guidelines to Selected Companies

Detailed applications of the guidelines derived from both the literature search and the Delphi study were covered in chapters 8, 9, and 10. The Bell Telephone Company's BISCUS/FACS information system was studied in light of these guidelines. In most instances, this system was found to have utilized the suggested criteria in the conceptual design phases. Highlighted in chapter 8 was the fact that the BISCUS/FACS system designers did everything that the experts felt was vital to designing a successful system.

Table 29.   Overall Comparison of Literature Search and Delphi.

Factor	% Discussing Factor	Delphi Ranking	Factor Ranked First in Delphi
FEASIBILITY STUDY			
Economic Feasibility	83%	3	User Involvement
REQUIREMENTS ANALYSIS			
Study of Present System	90%	3	User Involvement
SYSTEM SPECIFICATIONS			
Study of Output	76%	2	User
Input Specifications	76%	4	Involvement
Study of Data Flow	76%	5	
SYSTEM DESIGN			
Identification & Consideration of Needs	100%	1	Same
CODING & PROGRAMMING			
Standardization	86%	1	Same
TESTING			
Measurement through Testing	95%	2	Parallel
Planning for Testing	95%	3	Testing
DOCUMENTATION			
Completeness	100%	1	Same
Documenting Objectives	100%	not ranked	
Documenting Data Flow	100%		
IMPLEMENTATION			
Planning and Control	100%	2	User
Evaluation of System	100%	not ranked	Preparation

They also either added more depth in their application of these guidelines or actually carried the necessary steps further than the experts suggested.

In chapter 9, the American Airlines SABRE system was studied to see if these guidelines had been applied in the development of that management information system. Again, development had been more advanced than even the guidelines advocated. As pioneers in real-time systems, American Airlines has been the innovator for advocating many factors in these guidelines.

Chapter 10 examined the Weyerhaeuser system development to see if these guidelines had been utilized. Weyerhaeuser has applied many of the guidelines, but has a company philosophy that differs in some respects from the consensus obtained for the research. Indicative of company thinking was the comment of M.D. Robinson, a vice president of Weyerhaeuser: "Management information systems are not readily transferable. Each must be adopted to the needs of the user, and each is unique. Weyerhaeuser Company in many ways is more unique than anyone else" [160]. In spite of these slight differences, Weyerhaeuser has been quite successful in developing management information systems that do provide timely information in a usable form for management decisions.

These three companies are evidence of the selected guidelines having been used in successful management information systems. Although all three of the companies are slightly different in their managerial philosophy and in their organizational set-up, they have still used the majority of these guidelines in viable systems.

Conclusions

The original proposal was to construct a set of applicable guidelines, with emphasis on specific characteristics influencing success of a management information system. Such guidelines were to be selected so that they would be available for study, reference, comparison, and application for any company wishing to establish a successful management information system. Since a need for improvement in the conceptual design of MIS existed, this research report proposed to develop these selected guidelines.

The principal findings of this research were:

1. Common guidelines *do* exist and have been listed.

2. In listing the vital guidelines for developing a successful MIS, writers during the period from 1966 through 1976 have revealed a great deal of unanimity.

3. As shown in the results of the Delphi study, current writers and practitioners agree with the authors studied in the literature search as to the importance of these guidelines.

4. In developing viable management information systems, three companies with highly successful systems have applied the majority of these guidelines in their conceptual design.

12

Epilogue: Critical Factors of Conceptual Design in the 1980s

Most of the ideas presented in the previous chapter as conclusions about development of management information systems have carried over into the 1980s. Indeed, current thinking concerning conceptual design centers around the system development life cycle (SDLC) concept. As David Katch explained, "many installation managers have been forced to embrace the system life cycle as a basis for more effective utilization of their development resources" [109:xiii].

Although the phases included in this cycle vary from author to author, almost any author writing in the field of systems analysis and design since the 1970s agrees that such a cycle is necessary and valuable in considering system design problems. From the 1970s' list of eight, ten, or twelve stages or phases, the 1980 authors have condensed the phases to much smaller numbers—three or four phases seem to be the pattern. A closer look at these currently listed phases, however, reveals that the same ideas and concepts used in the 1970s still prevail.

As a pattern for discussion of how the 1980 authors think, Arthur Andersen & Company's model, Method/1, will be used. Writings of prominent authors will then be compared and contrasted with this popular SDLC.

Over a ten- to fifteen-year-period, Arthur Andersen has developed a method of analyzing and designing systems that has produced workable, effective information systems for their numerous clients. In solving the business problems for which this Big Eight accounting firm was hired, these systems have been both cost-effective and efficient [62:13].

Originally, the Arthur Andersen SDLC consisted of four primary phases: (1) Systems Planning; (2) Preliminary System Design; (3) System Installation; and (4) System Operation. As information has become more important and more available to businesses, the name of the first phase has been changed to "Information Planning," with the emphasis being on the final product, the "deliverable." Furthermore, as strategic planning has received recognition by businesses, this phase (strategic planning) has been added to the first step as a subset. Some writers even claim that strategic planning is a fifth phase [62:2].

E.G. Canning writes that Arthur Andersen has been developing "customized systems life cycle methodologies for clients for some twenty years." (*EDP Analyzer*, April 1985, p. 13). Method/1 has been developed as a structured project management and design methodology directed at helping companies complete the development of high quality systems on time and within budget. As members of this organization have gained experience in actually applying Method/1, the concepts are constantly being updated due to "experience gained from planning, designing, installing and maintaining information systems in almost every industry throughout the world" [62:3].

One of the goals of Method/1 is to meet the firm's information processing needs by enhancing management success, increasing productivity, and developing individual skills. Detailed planning to reduce problems, improved communications between end-users and information processing professionals, and strictly enforced project deadlines are all vehicles for insuring management success.

Through the improvement of effective user involvement in all aspects of systems planning and development, Method/1 may be used to increase productivity. Such planning and user involvement measurably reduce systems development start-up time, optimize available skills, and yield results of a higher quality. In keeping with current trends in system design, a project manager's workbench has been added to Method/1. This workbench

> provides the manager with automated planning tools to develop project work plans, to estimate projects, to develop project budgets, and to analyze the impact of various options. Control tools exist to track individual time, to report project results against budget, and to manage change requests. . . . [it] provides automated documentation facilities, for text, graphics and data. [*EDP Analyzer*, April 1985:13–14.]

By following the systematic approach to designing, Arthur Andersen has been quite successful in creating viable, efficient information systems to meet their client's needs. This workbench, DESIGN/1, measurably reduces the time necessary to analyze, design, and implement successful systems.

Now, with Method/1 as the standard for comparison and contrast, the thinking of current authors will be contrasted and compared with this particular SDLC methodology.

Raymond McLeod's Ideas

In his widely-used text, *MIS*, Raymond McLeod lists the phases of the SDLC as: (1) The Planning Phase; (2) The Analysis and Design Phase; (3) The Implementation Phase; and (4) Operations and Control. These four phases closely pattern themselves after the SDLC methodology proposed by Arthur Andersen & Company. Except for the semantics of using different names, the stages are essentially very similar. McLeod further emphasizes the important of the user by stating: "users of the information and the information specialists must work together" [McLeod:511].

David Kroenke's Opinions

In his elementary text, Kroenke lists seven steps, which include all the Arthur Andersen ideas separated into various stages: (1) Analyze feasibility; (2) Determine user requirements; (3) Specify alternatives; (4) Evaluate and select an alternative; (5) Design the system; (6) Develop and test; (7) Implement.

Parts of the first three steps would certainly be included in Information Planning. Certainly, a portion of (2), (3), and (4) would be a part of Preliminary System Design. Phases (6) and (7) replace the Installation Phase. Kroenke does not carry his discussion into the operational and maintenance phase.

Definitions of the meanings of these terms are quite similar, if not identical, to earlier explanations. Feasibility is again broken down into technical and cost feasibility. Kroenke, however, adds a new term "schedule feasibility" in lieu of the idea of whether or not the system "can" be designed. He comments: "If the computer system requires a year to develop, and if a solution must be found in six months, then the proposed system is infeasible" [Kroenke:98].

Burch, Strater, and Grudnitski's Presentations

John Burch and Felix Strater were among the original group of authors consulted for the information in chapter 5. In an updated version written with Gary Grudnitski, they follow the trend of shortening the number of phases in the SDLC by labeling their phases: (1) Systems Analysis (2) General Systems Design (3) Systems Evaluation and Justification (4) Detail Systems Design (5) Systems Implementation [34:248]. They state:

> The development of an information system, no matter what its size and complexity, requires many coordinated activities. The system development methodology is a standard

way to organize and coordinate these activities. The analyst who uses this methodology can apply it in any organization regardless of his or her expertise. [34:247]

George M. Scott's Concepts

George M. Scott writes, "The concept of the life cycle is central to systems investigations. Every system moves through several phases of a life cycle during its development" [170:454]. He then delineates two halves of the life cycle, calling them the Systems Investigation Phase and the Systems Maturity and Maintenance Phase. The first of these is really the life cycle as generally recognized, with Scott's phases being: Preliminary Survey, Analysis, Design, and Implementation. These almost duplicate the Method/1 model, although semantics differ.

The major idea presented in Scott's discussion is the importance of people in the successful implementation of information systems. Literature reveals that the failure to recognize the importance of interacting with the ultimate user of the system has been a primary cause of system failure in many organizations. Scott reiterates this idea by saying, "While technical tools are important, the most critical ingredient in systems investigation is the ability of people to work with other people" [170:454].

Scott later mentions that many people problems may be avoided if every person interested or involved in the system is consulted. He then states: "Systems personnel often err in not recognizing the participant's vested interested in the old system . . . A common error of the systems specialist is that of claiming the major share of credit for the new system" [170:460].

Emphasizing the importance of applying common sense, Scott writes: "While technical expertise is important, even more important to a systems investigation are diplomacy, tact, persuasiveness, sensitivity to people's needs, and concerns, and training in interview techniques." Scott is merely echoing the concerns given by numerous authors and also by the practitioners, the actual systems developers in the field.

What is surprising is that after ten to fifteen years of experience with systems development, such statements need to be made. Early systems failed because of neglect of the user, among other things. Even though the literature of the mid-1970s espoused these concepts and ideas, their importance and acceptance seem still to be neglected or ignored in the development of information systems. Continued emphasis on the importance of the individual and involvement of the users certainly should be stressed whenever the development of a system is discussed.

James O. Hicks' Discussion

Following the pattern originated by a noted practitioner, Tom DeMarco, James O. Hicks defines the "Classic Systems Development Life Cycle" as consisting of seven phases: (1) Feasibility Study; (2) Analysis; (3) Preliminary Design; (4) Hardware Study; (5) Detailed Design; (6) Coding and Testing; (7) Implementation; and (8) Auditing and Maintenance. These phases follow rather closely those listed in chapter 5, and the discussion and definition of these phases also parallels much of the previous discussion [89:326].

Hicks' addition is the introduction of structured techniques; he states that "designing a new system . . . is a relatively easy process" [89:354]. He then claims that the advantages of structured techniques are: (1) More work is done in the planning phase; (2) Such programs are easier to maintain; (3) Modules can be tested in a top-down fashion; and (4) Programs can be more easily understood [89:355]. All of these ideas are a part of the structured methodology previously discussed in chapter 4.

Since Hicks published his text in 1984, the sentences are filled with many of the current "buzz" words for systems analysis and design. One finds paragraphs describing data flow diagrams, decisions tables, data structure diagrams, structured walk-throughs, top-down coding, query languages, report generators, application generators, information centers, and decision support systems. Most of these concepts are widely accepted in the mid-1980s as being tools or methods that speed up the systems development life cycle.

Comparing the Old With The New

Regardless of which list of steps information specialists use, most development teams actually complete the checklists for analysis and design. The entire body of knowledge or methodology concerning systems analysis and design in 1985 is not very different from the situation in the 1970s. Different labels may be applied, but the definition of the concepts and the actual work involved are quite similar.

One key idea that Arthur Andersen system analysts propose, but that may not exactly be original with that company, is the fact that there really is not a mystique to systems development and design. Instead, there is an orderly manner of proceeding through the actual analysis and design. This method is not something that one must innately possess, such as the ability to draw or sing. It is a method that can be taught. Working with this concept in mind, Arthur Andersen has spent many years refining and improving their methodology and constantly updating it to include the latest innovations and discoveries.

Speeding Up Application Development

EDP Analyzer, in the April 1985 edition entitled "Speeding Up Application Development," tells how the classic systems development life cycle can be combined with newer concepts in systems design.

> Compress the product development life cycle! That is the battle cry in a growing number of industries. Getting an innovative, new product to market first is a key to gaining a competitive advantage. This speed-up push has serious repercussions for information systems departments, because more and more of the new products depend on an underlying computerized system. [p. 1]

Newer methods or tools that the designer and analyst may use to speed up the development process are mentioned.

Prototyping is the tool most often used to cut down on design time. However, the article suggests that neither the newer methods nor the SDLC should be used to the exclusion of the other.

> Not too long ago, two very different application development approaches were being touted for two quite different types of computer applications. The traditional project life cycle approach was judged best for production systems. And prototyping was declared best for ad hoc and decision support systems.
>
> Both approaches have their strengths and shortcomings. The question being asked today is: Can we somehow draw on both approaches for all application development, gaining the benefits of each and reducing the drawbacks of each? [pp. 4–5]

Listed were advantages of the SDLC as being a methodological development with defined milestones, deliverables, documentation and standards. Also, such systems have been found to be "robust and maintainable." A further advantage is that traditional systems have been dependable because of their machine-efficiency, with backup and recovery, checks and balances, and audit trails. SDLCs have also enabled both users and designers to gain the "big picture" and obtain an organization-wide view.

On the other hand, traditional systems have taken a very long time to develop. The user has not been involved — only sporadically during development, usually just at the beginning and at the end. Furthermore, when business conditions have changed during the traditional development, designers have found great difficulty in modifying the system to meet recently-discovered needs.

Much the converse is true of prototypes, which have primarily been used for one-time, ad hoc problems. They have been more haphazard, often "quick-and-dirty" little systems with little use of documentation, programming standards, and quality assurance. Quite often, these systems have stood alone and not been linked to other systems.

On the other hand, prototyping has brought about the fast development of systems, with iterative, new features added as the need arises. The development life cycle for prototypes is shorter, minimizing people resources, yet these systems are seldom developed with machine efficiency in mind.

The Best of Both Worlds

Currently, the best of both worlds is being considered by systems people. According to the *EDP Analyzer* [April 1985],

> We are seeing a convergence of the two, with a spectrum of approaches appearing. Information systems departments are experimenting with categorizing application requests in order to pick the most appropriate development methodology for each. . . . Companies are mixing and matching approaches—end user computing ideas are influencing mainline development practices and traditional development guidelines are being applied to user-developed systems. [p. 5]

No longer are prototyping and SDLC thought to be an either-or matter. Designers have asked "Why not combine the best of both?" Currently, designers are using prototyping to involve the user early and keep that user involved through the whole cycle, yet they also are following a systematic approach much like the SDLC. Both are needed before successful systems will evolve.

Summary

Through the use of prototyping, many companies are requiring the user to do more of the development work—about seventy percent in the case of Taco Bell [*EDP Analyzer*, April 1985, p. 2]. These companies still use the traditional project management, standard programming practices, and quality assurance guidelines. However, designers are combining these tried-and-true methods with newer ideas. Information center staff people supervise the user-developed systems and still follow the structured, systematic concepts of the traditional design approach. Merging these two approaches has sped up the design time and has actually led to a new development life cycle, with the still familiar phases or stages.

To improve the traditional method and to become cost-effective, designers are using prototyping, iterative development, and phased implementation. Application development tools, such as workbenches, aid in the speed-up process by automating parts of the projects. Combining both of these successful methods shows that information designers are responding to the challenge of new technology. At the same time, they are designing and delivering systems more quickly without sacrificing the efficiency, quality, and reliability of these systems.

Appendix

The Delphi Study

The Delphi process is a group method which utilizes written responses as opposed to bringing individuals together personally. Because this method does not require face-to-face contact, it is particularly useful for involving experts who cannot come together physically.

The participants in such a process should be recognized authorities in the field being researched. In addition, they should feel personally involved in the problem of concern, should have pertinent information to share, should be motivated to respond, and should feel that the results of the procedure will provide information that they value and to which they would not otherwise have access.

The method is essentially a series of questionnaires. The first questionnaire asks individuals to respond to a broad question. Each subsequent questionnaire is built upon responses to the preceding questionnaire. The process stops when consensus has been approached among participants.

Delphi Questionnaire #1

The initial conceptual design phase of information systems is a crucial part of the success of such systems.

Will you please list the things you consider to be *the* most vital or important in each of these parts of the design phase?

> Feasibility study
>
> Requirements analysis
>
> System specification
>
> System design
>
> Coding and programming
>
> Testing
>
> Documentation
>
> Implementation

Delphi Questionnaire #2

Listed on separate pages are the responses to the questions from the first Delphi mailing. Please do three things to these lists:

1. Review all items on each list. Comment, in one or two statements, on any item(s) you wish. You may argue in favor of an item, or request clarification. Brevity and clarity will facilitate analysis.

2. For each phase of the conceptual design, please select the *five* factors that you feel are the most important. Assign these values from 1 to 5, giving a "1" to the most important, etc. *This is merely a preliminary vote: it is not binding.*

3. Please return your response in the enclosed self-addressed, stamped envelope by June 15.

NOTE: In *any phase*, please feel free to add a category if you think it is more important than these listed.

QUESTIONNAIRE #2

I. FEASIBILITY STUDY

VOTE	FACTOR	SELECTED ORIGINAL COMMENTS	YOUR COMMENT
___	USER INVOLVEMENT	Heavy user participation--best if study is user-initiated with computer department acting as technical con-sultants	
		Study team consisting of highly respected individuals	
		User management willing to be involved	
___	STUDY OF CURRENT INFORMATION FLOW	Volume and complexity of processing	
		Obtaining accurate decision, information flow data, etc.	
		Identification of principal conceptual data bases necessary to support the system. Where data bases already exist in these data classes, the source, extent, and timeliness of existing data should be matched to anticipated needs.	
___	STUDY OF USER ATTITUDES AND EXPECTATIONS	Learning user expectations for a new system	
		Unreasonably optimistic estimates of system responsiveness should be avoided. Try to keep the "faddish" to a minimum. If a batch, 24-hour turnaround system will provide needed information in timely fashion for decision making, don't allow extensive discussions of on-line or rapid response batch capabilities.	
		Determining user attitude about information systems	
		Establishing a psychological contract with users	

QUESTIONNAIRE # 2

I. FEASIBILITY STUDY (cont)

VOTE	FACTOR	SELECTED ORIGINAL COMMENTS	YOUR COMMENT(S)
___	ECONOMIC FEASIBILITY	Economics. Can the objectives be met? Does it fit master plan?	
		An economic criteria of evaluation (except military, where benefits are non-economic)	
		Measurement of projected benefits--value of information to users (as well as direct and indirect costs	
		Potential gains from an MIS	
		If possible try to define a phased system with early phases providing benefits. No phase should require more than 1 year elapsed. Some phases may be needed to support data phases and benefits may be deferred to later phases.	
		The assessment of the technical feasibility of the proposed system and the economic justification or cost benefit from the proposed system	
___	STUDY OF PRESENT SYSTEM	Nature of the present management systems	
		Learning about the present system	
		The present organization	
___	TOP MANAGEMENT INVOLVEMENT	Proposal to management	
		Support at the highest levels in the organization	
		Top management support	

QUESTIONNAIRE #2

I. FEASIBILITY

VOTE	FACTOR	SELECTED ORIGINAL COMMENTS	YOUR COMMENT
	PLANNING FOR LONG RANGE	Clearly defined scope and objectives; written charter	
		Establishment of long range objectives and plans for the business is basic to establishing system plans and feasibility	
		A Global view of information rather than a parochial one is important. The scope of the proposed system and how it fits into the Information Systems Plan must be determined. Other organizations in the company who might potentially benefit should be consulted and, if possible, joint sponsorship encouraged.	

NOTE: Please feel free to add any factor you feel is more important than those listed

II. REQUIREMENTS ANALYSIS

VOTE	FACTOR	SELECTED ORIGINAL COMMENTS	YOUR COMMENT
___	COST VS. RESPONSE TIME	Estimated cost of MIS	
		Response time--cost and benefits of alternatives	
		Constraints or special requirements	
		Scope of hardware and software anticipated	
___	STUDY OF NEEDS	·Data collection & conversion that is required	
		Define structure of the reporting needs	
		Reports needed--triggered, demand, scheduled, planning, etc.	
		Initial implementation area as well as potential total requirements (all organizations and geographic) should be considered	
___	USER INVOLVEMENT	Involvement of users of information in specifying requirements	
		Leading users so that they actually design the system	
		Specification of the functions that the system must perform stated in terms of the user requirements	
		Iterative process involving information users participating in design sessions to set (and revise) system requirements	
		Obtaining full participation of users	

II. REQUIREMENTS ANALYSIS

VOTE	FACTOR	SELECTED ORIGINAL COMMENTS	YOUR COMMENT
____	STUDY OF CURRENT SYSTEM	Analysis of information needs of managers for planning and control in terms of summary reports, exception reports and "what if" queries.	
		First phase selected after feasibility definition--current system (manual or computerized) should be reviewed in detail. If at all possible try to get down to the original problem being addressed. More successful systems result if computer is used to help solve the problem rather than existing solution being mechanized	
		Transactions volume, by transactions type	
		Managerial effectiveness	
		System objectives. Information needs	
		"Owners" of data (i.e., the source of data) required should be identified	

NOTE: Please feel free to add any factor you think is more important than those listed

III. SYSTEM SPECIFICATIONS

VOTE	FACTOR	SELECTED ORIGINAL COMMENTS	YOUR COMMENT
___	DEVELOPING REQUIREMENTS	Developing an unambiguous plan	
		Configuration	
		Thorough definition	
		The requirements that the system must meet with respect to technical requirements such as file size, response time, etc.	
		Performance of system in terms of time, frequency and detail of information to be supplied	
		Fit of specifications and designs to structure defined above. Reporting framework dictates flow and timing in a successful system	
___	USER INVOLVEMENT	This should be the users' description of his needs	
		Personal interviews with data processing personnel	
		Involvement of users of information	
		Design sessions involving participation of information users	
		Holding complete and comprehensive reviews with users	
		Operational review of system specification with operating personnel	
___	OUTPUTS	Output requirements (<u>effective</u> output)	
		Design of output reports, including content and format	

III. SYSTEM SPECIFICATIONS (cont.)

VOTE	FACTOR	SELECTED ORIGINAL COMMENTS	YOUR COMMENT
___	INPUTS	Type of information to be supplied to each manager (inputs)	
		Inputs	
___	DATA FLOW	List of subsystems and inputs, outputs, and functions	
		Data flow	
		Computer Department assists by providing system analysis expertise in analyzing alternative work flows	
		No assumptions should be made about what the format of the computer solution	

___

NOTE: Please feel free to add any factor you think is more important than those listed

IV. SYSTEM DESIGN

VOTE	FACTOR	SELECTED ORIGINAL COMMENTS	YOUR COMMENT
___	INTEGRATED SYSTEM	Integrate system outputs into a hierarchy of reports, as well as source documents.	
		Objectives, constraints, information needs, information sources, output, file design.	
		Answer combined with system specifications: Fit of specifications and design to structure defined above. Reporting framework dictates flow and timing in successful system	
		For conceptual design, I consider the organization structure, the flow chart (or input/output matrix) representing approximate information inputs to managers and sources of information, the outline of the data base, and the scope of the electronic data processing system as most significant.	
___	CONSIDERATION OF THE DATA BASE	File organization and access method	
		Based on previous analysis--Logical Data Base needs are analyzed	
___	USER SUPPORT	Data Base support programs are designed	
		Existing Data Base support is matched to needs	

IV. SYSTEM DESIGN (cont.)

VOTE	FACTOR	SELECTED ORIGINAL COMMENTS	YOUR COMMENT
___	IDENTIFICATION & CONSIDERATION OF NEEDS	The system description in terms of runs, modules, flow of work, etc.	
		New requirements are fitted into appropriate Data Base or new Data Base established relative to total identified need.	
		Additional design sessions between study team and operating managers to review input requirements, processing, specifications, and output requirements.	
___	METHOD OF DESIGNING	Program module--definition of boundaries and interfaces	
		Top down design	
		Use of modern approaches to developing specifications: e.g., HIPO diagrams, modular programs, structured design, etc.	
___	BUILT-IN CONTROL	Control provisions to avoid unnecessary changes to "frozen" designs are needed	
		System effectiveness	
___			

NOTE: Please feel free to add any factor you feel is more important than those listed

V. CODING

VOTE	FACTOR	SELECTED ORIGINAL COMMENTS	YOUR COMMENTS
___	MODULAR	Clearly written modular code. The code should follow disciplined rules and use structured form Modular structure Top down--using modular approach	
___	STANDARDIZED	Use of standardized, meaningful variable names Extensive use of "Macro" techniques, common data definition section, etc. Record-code; single data input for multiple uses Structured programming using standard subset of high-level, program language	
___	ACCOMPANIED BY DOCUMENTATION	Use of standardized, extensive comments in coding Documentation (also project throughput) Thorough system documentation; clearly understood goals and objectives; clear coding standards	
___	ESTABLISHED GOALS FOR PROGRAMMER	Establishing clear goals for programmers	
___	TEST DATA DEVELOPMENT	Developing comprehensive test data independently of programmers	

V. CODING (cont.)

VOTE	FACTOR	SELECTED ORIGINAL COMMENTS	YOUR COMMENTS
___	NOT APPLICABLE TO CONCEPTUAL DESIGN	Part of detailed design and not relevant to conceptual design	
		Can't decide	
		Coding and testing can be combined in the conceptual design phase and will have little effect on the thinking at this stage. Once the system is designed and coding and testing can be properly estimated, their importance will increase significantly	
___	TEAM APPROACH	Chief programmer using librarian	
		Employing project management techniques	

NOTE: Please feel free to add any factor you feel is more important than those listed.

VI. TESTING

VOTE	FACTOR	SELECTED ORIGINAL COMMENTS	YOUR COMMENTS
———	PARALLEL	Run parallel systems (original & new) until problems resolved.	
		Parallel operations with "live" data	
		Desk-checking; parallel running and/or pilot testing	
———	INDEPENDENT DATA GENERATION	Standard prepared test data cases; prepared by suer with reference to system specifications, not be coder of modules	
		Independent test data generation	
		Sample data set testing	
———	MODULAR & INTEGRATIVE	A complete test of each module individually and combined plus the system in operation	
		Integrated testing from beginning--- one module at a time being added--- top down	
———	NOT RELEVANT TO CONCEPTUAL DESIGN	Coding and testing can be combined in the conceptual phase and will have very little effect on the thinking at this stage. Once the system is designed and coding and testing can be properly estimated, their importance will increase significantly	
		Not relevant to conceptual design	

VI. TESTING (cont.)

VOTE	FACTOR	SELECTED ORIGINAL COMMENTS	YOUR COMMENTS
___	TOP MANAGEMENT INVOLVEMENT	Understanding by top executives that testing may be a lengthy process	
___	MEASUREMENT OF SYSTEM THROUGH TESTING	Does it provide information needs? Will it perform as determined in feasibility study?	
		Use of evaluation tools to show areas requiring performance tuning prior to implementation	
		Completeness (Ashby's law of requisite variety)	
		Monitoring testing and keeping track of results	
___	PLANNING	Planning for testing	
___			

NOTE: Please feel free to add any factor you think is more important than those listed.

VII. DOCUMENTATION

VOTE	FACTOR	SELECTED ORIGINAL COMMENTS	YOUR COMMENTS
___	COMPLETENESS	A users' manual, an operator's manual, and a complete system document. The documentation should allow error-free maintenance of the system	
		Completeness	
		Develop complete documentation for users, designers, operators, etc.	
		Complete	
		Don't allow data processing personnel to "sign-off" on a system until documentation is <u>complete</u>.	
___	INFORMATION FLOW DOCUMENTATION	Use of HIPO diagrams down through "program" level only. Modified HIPO used to document modules	
		Throughput project	
		Conceptual design level flow chart of information flows to managers	
___	DATA BASE DOCUMENTATION	Outline of data base (organization of files and size)	
		Data base documentation standardized provided separate from "application" documents	

VII. DOCUMENTATION

VOTE	FACTOR	SELECTED ORIGINAL COMMENTS	YOUR COMMENTS
___	DOCUMENTATION FOR USER	User-oriented materials as well as systems-oriented	
		User documentation should be prepared by user department	
		Detailed documentation should be computer readable for use of updating	
___	OBJECTIVES DOCUMENTED	Description of objectives of the MIS, the organization and subsystems	
		Document measurable objectives of the system as well as data-information flows	
		Estimate of cost of MIS installation and operation and of benefits from improved decision making and improved system efficiency	
___	CONTINUOUS DOCUMENTATION	Document step by step as accomplished. Documentation cannot be left to the end or it will never be accomplished	

NOTE: Please feel free to add any factor you think is more important than those listed.

VIII. IMPLEMENTATION

VOTE

FACTOR

____ USER PREPARATION

SELECTED ORIGINAL COMMENTS	YOUR COMMENT

Adequate change procedures to train users, overcome hostility, and make corrective changes as required

The entire process of design should be focused on implementation.

If you are speaking of "installation and conversion", then user preparation is the key. Training should be thorough and documentation ready to go.

Training and cooperation of users. No matter how well the system is designed and built, ultimate success will depend on acceptance by the users. Their acceptance can depend a great deal on the amount of their input to the conceptual and detail design phases of the project.

Provide training facilities and consideration during implementation phases (e.g., if extensive format changes and additional input editing is occurring-- don't expect initial reject volumes to be as low as they will be after system has been installed for over a year).

____ TOP MANAGEMENT SUPPORT

Top management support through the actual use of the system in regular and ongoing operating-managerial activities (vs. simply supporting it)

VIII. IMPLEMENTATION

VOTE	FACTOR	SELECTED ORIGINAL COMMENTS	YOUR COMMENT
___	NOT RELEVANT	Not relevant to conceptual design	
___	CAPABILITY FOR HANDLING PROBLEMS	Prompt reaction to performance problems--adequate diagnostic tools to identify module or data base causing bottleneck	
___	PHASED IMPLEMENTATION	Provide for phased installation	
		Expect a "learning curve" for users and computer operators. A system tuned for ultimate stable environment may crater during implementation (e.g., online application which is first implemented in the field will have transaction rate 2 to 3 times production volume as "novelty" wears off)	
___	PARALLEL	Provide for adequate parallel period during which old system and new system are both 100% active	
___	EVALUATION	User acceptance in accordance with PREDETERMINED acceptance tests	
		Evaluation of system effectiveness (?)	
___	PLANNING & CONTROL	Use work breakdown structure and some form of planning and control such as PERT	
		A thorough implementation plan that spells out implementation times and cost elements	

VIII. IMPLEMENTATION

VOTE   FACTOR   YOUR COMMENT

NOTE: Please feel free
to add any factor you feel
is more important than
those listed

Delphi Questionnaire #3 (Final Round)

Listed on separate pages are the responses to the questions from the first and second Delphi mailings. These responses are now listed in the composite order of importance you placed on these factors.

Please do three things to these lists:

1. Review all of the items on each list (several have been added from the second Delphi mailing), along with the comments presented. Comment, in one or two statements, on any item(s) you wish.

2. Now that you have reviewed these facets, along with those added in Round Two, please select the *five* factors you feel are the most important to each of the phases of the conceptual design, ranking these from "1" to "5".

3. Please return your response in the enclosed self-addressed, stamped envelope by August 5.

General Comments about the Survey

For the first round of the Delphi, several of you talked with me by phone and expressed your difficulty in delineating the categories as I had arbitrarily selected them. However, even though you felt that many of them did overlap, you answered the questions as asked.

From the second round, one noted author expressed the same sentiments. These are lucid and valid, and are given in depth here:

I had difficulty because categories overlap. See the comments you provided. Why not have experts rate the major phases as well? (e.g. (1) Coding can be (is) considered part of implementation (by many experts). (2) What is meant by "Requirements Analysis (RA)" particularly as contrasted to "SS — System Specifications?" To me, they are quite different, but your arrangement does not capture that difference. RA means what the system must be capable of doing in the form of tasks and volumes. SS relates to technical (storage and retrieval, for example) capabilities of the system. RA sets objectives but SS states physical characteristics of the hardware for the system.

A major weakness of MIS research to date is the failure to set unambiguous definitions on concepts and terms so that meaningful analysis is possible. A few glaring examples here: Information = ? Input = ? Output = ? MIS = ?

Others of you questioned the order of the phases, feeling that specifications should follow design rather than precede it.

SUMMARIZED ANSWERS TO QUESTIONNAIRE #3

Note: These are listed in the composite order of importance
       assigned from Questionnaire #2. Factors have been
       added to several categories

I. FEASIBILITY STUDY

_____   USER INVOLVEMENT

_____   TOP MANAGEMENT INVOLVEMENT

_____   ECONOMIC FEASIBILITY

_____   STUDY OF USER ATTITUDES & EXPECTATIONS

_____   PLANNING FOR LONG RANGE

_____   STUDY OF CURRENT INFORMATION FLOW

_____   STUDY OF PRESENT SYSTEM

Added Factors:

_____   OPERATIONAL FEASIBILITY

_____   TECHNICAL FEASIBILITY

II. REQUIREMENTS ANALYSIS

_____   USER INVOLVEMENT

_____   STUDY OF (USER) NEEDS

_____   STUDY OF CURRENT SYSTEM

_____   COST VS. RESPONSE TIME

Added Factors:

_____   SPECIFY SHORT-RUN & LONG-RUN REQUIREMENTS

_____   IMPROVE CONTROL

_____   LIMITS TO COST

_____   ECONOMIC ANALYSIS

_____   IMPROVEMENT IN MANAGERIAL CONTROL

_____   REPORTS--MODE & LEVEL OF AGGREGATION

SUMMARIZED ANSWERS TO QUESTIONNAIRE #3 (cont.)

III. SYSTEM SPECIFICATIONS

    _____ USER INVOLVEMENT

    _____ OUTPUTS

    _____ DEVELOPING REQUIREMENTS

    _____ INPUTS

    _____ DATA FLOW

Added Factors:

    _____ SYSTEM CHART

    _____ FILE DESIGN

    _____ DATA CODING SYSTEM

IV. SYSTEM DESIGN

    _____ IDENTIFICATION & CONSIDERATION OF NEEDS

    _____ INTEGRATED SYSTEM

    _____ CONSIDERATION OF THE DATA BASE

    _____ METHOD OF DESIGNING

    _____ USER SUPPORT

    _____ BUILT IN CONTROL

Added Factors:

    _____ HARDWARE & SOFTWARE

    _____ DATA CODING SYSTEM

SUMMARIZED ANSWERS TO QUESTIONNÀIRE #3 (cont.)

V.   CODING

     _____   STANDARDIZED

     _____   MODULAR

     _____   ACCOMPANIED BY DOCUMENTATION

     _____   ESTABLISHED GOALS FOR PROGRAMMERS

     _____   TEST DATA DEVELOPMENT

     _____   TEAM APPROACH

     _____   NOT APPLICABLE TO CONCEPTUAL DESIGN

Added Factor:

     _____   INTEGRATION OF CODE NUMBERS INTO A
                       TOTAL SYSTEM OF CODES

VI.   TESTING

     _____   PARALLEL

     _____   MEASUREMENT OF SYSTEM THROUGH TESTING

     _____   MODULAR & INTEGRATIVE

     _____   PLANNING

     _____   INDEPENDENT DATA GENERATION

     _____   TOP MANAGEMENT INVOLVEMENT

     _____   NOT RELEVANT TO CONCEPTUAL DESIGN

Added Factor:

     _____   PREIMPLEMENTATION & POSTIMPLEMENTATION TESTING

SUMMARIZED ANSWERS TO QUESTIONNAIRE #3 (cont.)

VII. <u>DOCUMENTATION</u>

    _____   DOCUMENTATION FOR USER

    _____   COMPLETENESS

    _____   CONTINUOUS DOCUMENTATION

    _____   OBJECTIVES DOCUMENTED

    _____   INFORMATION FLOW DOCUMENTATION

    _____   DATA BASE DOCUMENTATION

<u>Added Factor</u>:

    _____   STANDARDIZED

VIII. <u>IMPLEMENTATION</u>

    _____   USER PREPARATION

    _____   CAPABILITY FOR HANDLING PROBLEMS

    _____   EVALUATION

    _____   PLANNING & CONTROL

    _____   TOP MANAGEMENT SUPPORT

    _____   PARALLEL

    _____   PHASED IMPLEMENTATION

    _____   NOT RELEVANT

I. FEASIBILITY STUDY   QUESTIONNAIRE #3   1

VOTE	FACTOR	SELECTED ORIGINAL COMMENTS	COMMENTS FROM SECOND DELPHI
———	USER INVOLVEMENT	Heavy user participation--best if study is user-initiated with computer department acting as technical consultants.	Some rankings are very close.
		Study team consisting of highly respected individuals.	The system will need to belong to the user if it is to be successful. This should be the goal from the beginning.
		User management willing to be involved.	
———	TOP MANAGEMENT INVOLVEMENT	Proposal to management	If we mean MIS, top management must feel the need for a better system.
		Support at the highest levels in the organization.	For an information system, management is the user! Top management needs to realize and support this.
		Top management support	When feasible an Information System Plan should be established and approved by Executive Management

I. FEASIBILITY STUDY (cont.)   QUESTIONNAIRE #3   2

VOTE	FACTOR	SELECTED ORIGINAL COMMENTS	COMMENTS FROM SECOND DELPHI
___	ECONOMIC FEASIBILITY	Economics: Can the objectives be met? Does it fit master plan?	This deals primarily with cost of development, implementation and operation. Measurement of benefits is difficult. One corporate executive said, "If you can measure the dollar benefit, it isn't an MIS."
		An economic criteria of evaluation (except military, where benefits are non-economic).	
		Measurement of projected benefits--- value of information to users (as well as direct and indirect costs).	Many systems are justified on intangible benefits which are impossible to quantify in dollars and cents. Where possible economic savings is the best selling tool but is not absolutely necessary in all cases.
		Potential gains from an MIS.	
		If possible try to define a phased system with early phases providing benefits. No phase should require more than 1 year elapsed. Some phases may be needed to support data phases and benefits may be deferred to later phases.	
		The assessment of the technical feasibility of the proposed system and the economic justification or cost benefit from the proposed system.	Economic and technical feasibility are not the same.

I. FEASIBILITY STUDY (cont.)   QUESTIONNAIRE #3   3

VOTE	FACTOR	SELECTED ORIGINAL COMMENTS	COMMENTS FROM SECOND DELPHI
___	STUDY OF USER ATTITUDES & EXPECTATIONS	Learning user expectations for a new system.	Subsumed under "USER INVOLVEMENT."
		Unreasonably optimistic estimates of system responsiveness should be avoided. Try to keep the "faddish" to a minimum. If a batch, 24-hour turnaround system will provide needed information in timely fashion for decision making, don't allow extensive discussions of on-line or rapid response batch capabilities.	
		Determining user attitude about information systems.	
		Establishing a psychological contract with users.	
___	PLANNING FOR LONG RANGE	Clearly defined scope and objectives; written charter.	A deficiency of many MIS is that they are patched together to solve short range operating problems.
		Establishment of long range objectives and plans for the business is basic to establishing system plans and feasibility.	
		A Global view of information rather than a parochial one is important. The scope of the proposed system and how it fits into the Information Systems Plan must be determined. Other organizations in the company who might potentially benefit should be consulted and, if possible, joint sponsorship encouraged.	Agree

I. FEASIBILITY STUDY (cont.)   QUESTIONNAIRE #3   4

VOTE	FACTOR	SELECTED ORIGINAL COMMENTS	COMMENTS FROM SECOND DELPHI
___	STUDY OF CURRENT INFORMATION FLOW	Volume and complexity of processing Obtaining accurate decision, information flow data, etc. Identification of principal conceptual data bases necessary to support the system. Where data bases already exist in these data classes; the source, extent, and timeliness of existing data should be matched to anticipated needs.	At the conceptual stage, this factor as described either is too detailed or tends to lock you into the past. Easily can confuse data flow with information flow. An Information Systems Network should be prepared to analyze all information requirements so that the place of this system is well established in the total environment.
___	STUDY OF PRESENT SYSTEM	Nature of the present management systems. Learning about the present system. The present organization.	Company organization, problem areas, lack of information flow for major decisions. Same as "STUDY OF CURRENT INFORMATION FLOW."
Added Factors:			
___	OPERATIONAL FEASIBILITY		
___	TECHNICAL FEASIBILITY		

II. REQUIREMENTS ANALYSIS   QUESTIONNAIRE #3   5

VOTE	FACTOR	SELECTED ORIGINAL COMMENTS	COMMENTS FROM SECOND DELPHI
___	USER INVOLVEMENT	Involvement of users of information in specifying requirements.	Again, user is management for an <u>information</u> system.
		Leading users so that they actually design the system.	
		Specification of the functions that the system must perform stated in terms of the user requirements.	
		Iterative process involving information users participating in design sessions to set (and revise) system requirements.	
		Obtaining full participation of users.	
___	STUDY OF (USER) NEEDS	Data collection & conversion that is required.	
		Define structure of the reporting needs.	
		Reports needed --triggered, demand, scheduled, planning, etc.	
		Initial implementation areas as well as potential total requirements (all organizations and geographic) should be considered.	

II. REQUIREMENTS ANALYSIS (cont.)   QUESTIONNAIRE #3

6

VOTE	FACTOR	SELECTED ORIGINAL COMMENTS	COMMENTS FROM SECOND DELPHI
___	STUDY OF CURRENT SYSTEM	Analysis of information needs of managers for planning and control in terms of summary reports, exception reports, and "what if" queries.	Suggested new title: "STUDY OF CURRENT SYSTEM TO OBTAIN VOLUMES & TIMING REQUIREMENTS
		First phase selected after feasibility definition--current system (manual or computerized) should be reviewed in detail. If at all possible try to get down to the original problem being addressed. More successful systems result if computer is used to help solve the problem rather than existing solution being mechanized.	This is "needs."
			Should this item be "STUDY OF CURRENT MANAGEMENT SYSTEM"?
		Transactions volume, by transactions type.	
		Managerial effectiveness.	
		System objectives. Information needs.	
		"Owners" of data (i.e., the source of data) required should be identified	
___	COST VERSUS RESPONSE TIME	Estimated cost of MIS	Response time is not the only (or always the best) measure of benefits.
		Response time--cost and benefits of alternatives	
		Constraints or special requirements.	Cost and response times should be separated
		Scope of hardware and software anticipated	Should this item be under "FEASIBILITY STUDY?"

II. REQUIREMENTS ANALYSIS (cont.)   QUESTIONNAIRE #3

7

VOTE	FACTOR	SELECTED ORIGINAL COMMENTS	COMMENTS FROM SECOND DELPHI
	Added Factors:		
___	SPECIFY SHORT-RUN & LONG-RUN REQUIREMENTS		
___	IMPROVE CONTROL		
___	LIMITS TO COST		This author separated "Cost" from "Response Time."
___	ECONOMIC ANALYSIS		
___	IMPROVEMENT IN MANAGERIAL CONTROL		This is not just speeding feedback, but getting effective feedback in real-time.
___	REPORTS--MODE & LEVEL OF AGGREGATION		Should reports be printouts, typed, CRT, or formal oral reports at staff meetings? The level of aggregation is related to the number of reports prepared. One encyclopedia could serve everyone and so could several hundred tailored-to-each-manager reports. In between, we will find the kind and number of useful reports.

III. SYSTEM SPECIFICATIONS   QUESTIONNAIRE #3

8

VOTE	FACTOR	SELECTED ORIGINAL COMMENTS	COMMENTS FROM SECOND DELPHI
___	USER INVOLVEMENT	This should be the users' description of his needs.	
		Personal interviews with data processing personnel.	
		Involvement of users of information.	
		Design sessions involving participation of information users.	
		Holding complete and comprehensive reviews with users.	
		Operational review of system specification with operating personnel.	
___	OUTPUTS	Output requirements (effective outputs).	Frequency should be included.
		Design of output reports, including content and format	Inquiry capabilities

III. SYSTEM SPECIFICATIONS (cont.)   <u>QUESTIONNAIRE #3</u>

9

VOTE	FACTOR	SELECTED ORIGINAL COMMENTS	COMMENTS FROM SECOND DELPHI
___	DEVELOPING REQUIREMENTS	Developing an unambiguous plan.	This topic is too vague. Requirements is practically synonymous with performance specs.
		Configuration.	
		The requirements that the system must meet with respect to technical requirements such as file size, response time, etc.	Should this item be under "REQUIREMENTS ANALYSIS?"
		Performance of system in terms of time, frequency and detail of information to be supplied.	This represents performance specs. Add other items relating to who is to be served.
		Fit of specifications and designs to structure defined above. Reporting framework dictates flow and timing in a successful system.	
___	INPUTS	Type of information to be supplied.	This is an <u>output</u> of the system. <u>Inputs</u> are items of data.
		Inputs.	This seems to be an <u>output</u>.

III. SYSTEM SPECIFICATIONS (cont.)   QUESTIONNAIRE #3   10

VOTE	FACTOR	SELECTED ORIGINAL COMMENTS	COMMENTS FROM SECOND DELPHI
___	DATA FLOW	List of subsystems and inputs, outputs, and functions.	As a performance spec. this item, data flow, should be described in terms of what is to be expected of it.
		Data flow.	
		Computer Department assists by providing system analysis expertise in analyzing alternative work flows.	
		No assumptions should be made about what the format of the computer solution.	
Added Factors:			
___	SYSTEM CHART		General design of system and its interfaces with other systems. Not just lists, but a flowchart indicating storage media, access, etc.
___	FILE DESIGN		Specify file contents, format, logical structure, etc.
___	DATA CODING SYSTEM		

IV. SYSTEM DESIGN

QUESTIONNAIRE #3

11

VOTE	FACTOR	SELECTED ORIGINAL COMMENTS	COMMENTS FROM SECOND DELPHI
___	IDENTIFICATION & CONSIDERATION OF NEEDS	The system description in terms of runs, modules, flow of work, etc. New requirements are fitted into appropriate Data Base or new Data Base established relative to total identified need. Additional design sessions between study team and operating managers to review input requirements, processing, specifications and output requirements.	Part of an "integrated system."
___	INTEGRATED SYSTEM	Integrate system outputs into a hierarchy of reports, as well as source documents. Objectives, constraints, information needs, information sources, output, file design. Answer combined with "System Specifications." Fit of specifications and design to structure defined above. Reporting framework dictates flow and timing in successful system. For conceptual design, I consider the organization structure, the flow chart (or input/output matrix) representing approximate information inputs to managers and sources of information, the outline of the data base, and the scope of the electronic data processing system as most significant.	

IV. SYSTEM DESIGN (cont.) QUESTIONNAIRE #3 12

VOTE	FACTOR	SELECTED ORIGINAL COMMENTS	COMMENTS FROM SECOND DELPHI
	CONSIDERATION OF THE DATA BASE	File organization and access method. / Based on previous analysis--Logical Data Base needs are analyzed.	
	METHOD OF DESIGNING	Program module--definition of boundaries and interfaces. / Top-down design / Use of modern approaches to developing specifications: e.g., HIPO diagrams, modular programs, structured design, etc.	
	USER SUPPORT	Data Base support programs are designed. / Existing Data Base support is matched to needs.	
	BUILT IN CONTROL	Control provisions to avoid unnecessary changes to "frozen" designs are needed. / System effectiveness.	
Added Factors:			
	HARDWARE & SOFTWARE		
	DATA CODING SYSTEM		

QUESTIONNAIRE #3

13

V. CODING

VOTE	FACTOR	SELECTED ORIGINAL COMMENTS	COMMENTS FROM SECOND DELPHI
			GENERAL COMMENTS ABOUT CODING:
			Rankings apply to coding considerations as they will be applied. Again, these are secondary considerations in the conceptual design phase.
			Categories under "Coding" are not helpful.
			Not familiar enough to estimate.
___	STANDARDIZED	Use of standardized, meaningful variable names.	Must have all of these [modular, standardized, accompanied by documentation].
		Extensive use of "Macro" techniques, common data definition section, etc.	
		Record-code; single data input for multiple uses.	
		Structured programming using standard subset of high-level, program language.	
___	MODULAR	Clearly written modular code. The code should follow disciplined rules and use structured form.	Must have all of these [modular, standardized, accompanied by documentation].
		Modular structure.	
		Top down--using modular approach.	

QUESTIONNAIRE #3

14

V. CODING

VOTE	FACTOR	SELECTED ORIGINAL COMMENTS	COMMENTS FROM SECOND DELPHI
	ACCOMPANIED BY DOCUMENTATION	Use of standardized, extensive comments in coding.	Must have all of these [modular, standardized, accompanied by documentation.]
		Documentation (also project throughput).	
		Thorough system documentation; clearly understood goals and objectives; clear coding standards.	
	ESTABLISHED GOALS FOR PROGRAMMERS	Establishing clear goals for programmers.	
	TEST DATA DEVELOPMENT	Developing comprehensive test data independently of programmers.	
	TEAM APPROACH	Chief programmer using librarian.	Implicit in above comments or factors.
		Employing project management techniques.	

QUESTIONNAIRE #3

15

V. CODING (cont.)

VOTE	FACTOR	SELECTED ORIGINAL COMMENTS	COMMENTS FROM SECOND DELPHI
___	NOT APPLICABLE TO CONCEPTUAL DESIGN.	Part of detailed design and not relevant to conceptual design.	
		Can't decide.	
		Coding and testing can be combined in the conceptual design phase and will have little effect on the thinking at this stage. Once the system is designed and coding and testing can be properly estimated, their importance will increase significantly.	

Added Factor:

| ___ | INTEGRATION OF CODE NUMBERS INTO A TOTAL SYSTEM OF CODES | | |

16

QUESTIONNAIRE #3

VI. TESTING

VOTE	FACTOR	SELECTED ORIGINAL COMMENTS	COMMENTS FROM SECOND DELPHI
			GENERAL COMMENT ABOUT TESTING
			Rankings are for testing considerations at the proper time of application. As with "CODING," this is a secondary consideration of Conceptual Design.
	PARALLEL	Run parallel systems (original and new) until problems resolved.	Unless the old and new systems are very similar, this probably is not practical. If the systems are very similar, the goals of the new system probably were not attained.
		Parallel operations with "live" data.	
		Desk-checking; parallel running and/or pilot testing.	
	MEASUREMENT OF SYSTEM THROUGH TESTING	Does it provide information needs? Will it perform as determined in feasibility study?	
		Use of evaluation tools to show areas requiring performance tuning prior to implementation	
		Completeness (Ashby's law of requisite variety).	
		Monitoring testing and keeping track of results.	

VI. TESTING (cont.)

QUESTIONNAIRE #3

17

VOTE	FACTOR	SELECTED ORIGINAL COMMENTS	COMMENTS FROM SECOND DELPHI
___	MODULAR & INTEGRATIVE	A complete test of each module individually and combined plus the system in operation. Integrated testing from beginning---one module at a time being added---top-down.	
___	PLANNING	Planning for testing	Implicit in above factors.
___	INDEPENDENT DATA GENERATION	Standard prepared test data cases; prepared by user with reference to system specifications, not by coder of modules. Independent test data generation. Sample data set testing.	
___	TOP MANAGEMENT INVOLVEMENT	Understanding by top executives that testing may be a lengthy process.	

QUESTIONNAIRE #3

18

VI. TESTING (cont.)

VOTE	FACTOR	SELECTED ORIGINAL COMMENTS	COMMENTS FROM SECOND DELPHI
___	NOT RELEVANT TO CONCEPTUAL DESIGN	Coding and testing can be combined in the conceptual phase and will have very little effect on the thinking at this stage. Once the system is designed and coding and testing can be properly estimated, their importance will increase significantly.	
		Not relevant to conceptual design.	

Added Factor:

___	PREIMPLEMENTA- TION AND POST- IMPLEMENTATION TESTING		

VII. DOCUMENTATION

QUESTIONNAIRE #3

19

VOTE	FACTOR	SELECTED ORIGINAL COMMENTS	COMMENTS FROM SECOND DELPHI
			GENERAL COMMENTS FOR DOCUMENTATION
			Data base documentation and information flow must be involved for completeness.
			I really see these factors [Information Flow, Data Base Documentation for User] as a part of the "completeness" factor.
___	DOCUMENTATION FOR USER	User-oriented materials as well as systems-oriented. User documentation should be prepared by user department. Detailed documentation should be computer readable for use of updating.	
___	COMPLETENESS	A users' manual, an operator's manual, and a complete system document. The documentation should allow error-free maintenance of the system. Completeness. Develop complete documentation for users, designers, operators, etc. Don't allow data processing personnel to "sign-off" on a system until documentation is complete.	

20

VII. DOCUMENTATION (cont.)

QUESTIONNAIRE #3

VOTE	FACTOR	SELECTED ORIGINAL COMMENTS	COMMENTS FROM SECOND DELPHI
___	CONTINUOUS DOCUMENTATION	Document step by step as accomplished. Documentation cannot be left to the end or it will never be accomplished.	
___	OBJECTIVES DOCUMENTED	Description of objectives of the MIS, the organization and subsystems.	
		Document measurable objectives of the system as well as data-information flows.	
		Estimate of cost of MIS installation and operation and of benefits from improved decision making and improved system efficiency.	
___	INFORMATION FLOW DOCUMENTATION	Use of HIPO diagrams down through "program" level only. Modified HIPO used to document modules.	Must be involved for completeness.
		Throughput project.	
		Conceptual design level flow chart of information flows to managers.	

VII. DOCUMENTATION (cont.)   QUESTIONNAIRE #3   21

VOTE	FACTOR	SELECTED ORIGINAL COMMENTS	COMMENTS FROM SECOND DELPHI
____	DATA BASE DOCUMENTATION	Outline of data base (organization of files and size). Data base documentation standardized provided separate from "application" documents.	Must be involved for completeness.
	Added Factor:		
____	STANDARDIZED		

QUESTIONNAIRE #3

22

VIII. IMPLEMENTATION

VOTE	FACTOR	SELECTED ORIGINAL COMMENTS	COMMENTS FROM SECOND DELPHI
			GENERAL COMMENT ON IMPLEMENTATION:
			This is also a secondary consideration during conceptual design.
	USER PREPARATION	Adequate change procedures to train users, overcome hostility, and make corrective changes as required.	
		The entire process of design should be focused on implementation.	
		If you are speaking of "installation and conversion," then user preparation is the key. Training should be thorough and documentation ready to go.	
		Training and cooperation of users. No matter how well the system is designed and built, ultimate success will depend on acceptance by the users. Their acceptance can depend a great deal on the amount of their input to the conceptual and detail design phases of the project.	
		Provide training facilities and considerations during implementation phases (e.g., if extensive format changes and additional input editing is occurring--- don't expect initial reject volumes to be as low as they will be after the system has been installed for over a year.	

VIII. IMPLEMENTATION   QUESTIONNAIRE #3   23

VOTE	FACTOR	SELECTED ORIGINAL COMMENTS	COMMENTS ON SECOND DELPHI
____	CAPABILITY FOR HANDLING PROBLEMS	Prompt reaction to performance problems --adequate diagnostic tools to identify module or data base causing bottleneck.	
____	EVALUATION	User acceptance in accordance with PREDETERMINED acceptance tests. Evaluation of system effectiveness (?).	Evaluation of problems involved in implementation. Post audit. A part of "control" factor below.
____	PLANNING & CONTROL	Use work breakdown structure and some form of planning and control such as PERT. A thorough implementation plan that spells out implementation times and cost elements.	

QUESTIONNAIRE #3

24

VIII. IMPLEMENTATION

VOTE	FACTOR	SELECTED ORIGINAL COMMENTS	COMMENTS ON SECOND DELPHI
___	TOP MANAGEMENT SUPPORT	Top management support through the actual use of the system in regular and ongoing operating-managerial activities (vs. simply supporting it).	
___	PARALLEL	Provide for adequate parallel period during which old system and new system are both 100% active.	May not be possible due to difference of systems. See Category VI.
___	PHASED IMPLEMENTATION	Provide for phased installation. Expect a "learning curve" for users and computer operators. A system tuned for ultimate stable environment may crater during implementation (e.g., online application which is first implemented in the field will have transaction rate two to three times production volume as "novelty" wears off).	
___	NOT RELEVANT	Not relevant to conceptual design.	

Bibliography

Books and Journals

[1]   Abraham, K. V. "The Evolution of Management Science and the Planning Functions and Their Relations to MIS." *Proceedings Third Annual Conference, Society for MIS, Denver Colorado, September 1971.* Chicago: The Society for Management Information Systems, 1971.

[2]   Ackoff, Russell L. "Management Misinformation Systems." *Management Science,* vol. 14, no. 4 (December 1967), pp. 18–25.

[3]   "Airlines in Turmoil." *Business Week* (October 10, 1983), pp. 98–102.

[4]   Alexander, M. J. *Information Systems Analysis: Theory and Applications.* Chicago: Science Research Associates, Inc., 1974.

[5]   American Airlines. *Introduction to SABRE, 1963.* New York: American Airlines Intracompany Publication, 1963.

[6]   ———. *Programming Standards Manual.* New York: American Airlines Intracompany Publication, 1963.

[7]   "American Airlines Wing toward Record High Net." *Barrons,* vol. 45 (December 6, 1965), p. 21.

[8]   "American Promotes Its Kiwis." *Sales Management,* vol. 113 (July 22, 1974), p. 3.

[9]   "American Sets Freight Push." *Advertising Age,* vol. 44. (May 7, 1973), p. 40.

[10]   Anderson, David R. and Thomas A. Williams. "Viewing MIS from the Top." *Journal of Systems Management,* vol. 24, no. 7 (July 1973), pp. 21–24.

[11]   Anderson, Howard. "IBM's Telecom Strategy." *Telephony,* vol. 194, no. 14 (April 3, 1978), pp. 34–36.

[12]   Aron, J. D. "Information Systems in Perspective." *Computing Surveys,* vol. 1, no. 4 (December 1969), pp. 214–36.

[13]   Association for Systems Management. *Business Systems.* Cleveland, Ohio: Association for Systems Management, 1974.

[14]   Astrahan, M. M. "Automated Library Soon?" *Machine Design,* vol. 30 (June 1958), p. 41.

[15]   Aswen, D. L. "Why We Are Using an Automatic Data Collection System." *Power Industry,* vol. 74 (March 1958), p. 9.

[16]   Athey, Thomas H. *Systematic Systems Approach.* Englewood Cliffs, New Jersey: Prentice-Hall, 1982.

[17]   "AT&T Divestiture & Industry Deregulation." Pennsauken, New Jersey: Auerbach Publications, 1985, pp. 1–8.

[18]   "AT&T Pushes Unix Forward." *Datapro Small Computer News* (May 1985), p. 1.

[19]   Axelrod, C. Warren. "The New Economics of Computers." *Infosystems*, vol. 32, no. 6 (June 1985), pp. 66–68.

[20]   Babb, Elizabeth A. "Increasing Productivity with the Application Generator Interface." *Journal of Information Systems Management*, vol. 2, no. 2 (Spring 1985), pp. 57–67.

[21]   Ball, Susan R. and Lawrence M. Light. "Systems Development: Finding the Right Path." *ICP Data Processing Management*, vol. 9, no. 1 (Spring 1984), pp. 30–32.

[22]   Bass, Leonard J. "A Generalized User Interface for Applications Programs (II)." *Communications of the ACM*, vol. 28, no. 6 (June 1985), pp. 617–27.

[23]   Blumenthal, Sherman C. *Management Information Systems*. Englewood Cliffs, New Jersey: Prentice-Hall, 1969.

[24]   Bosworth, George H. "Managing a Programmer Shortage." *Datamation*, vol. 29, no. 8 (August 1983), pp. 139–44.

[25]   Boyd, Kenneth. "Information Systems for Management: Real-World Interaction with Computer-based Technology." *Information Systems for Management*. Englewood Cliffs, New Jersey: Prentice-Hall, 1972, pp. 23–41.

[26]   Brabb, George J. *Computer and Information Systems in Business*. Boston, Massachusetts: Houghton Mifflin, 1976.

[27]   "The Brassiest Bell Company." *Business Week* (March 14, 1983), pp. 120–124.

[28]   "Breaking Up the Phone Company." *Fortune*, vol. 107, no. 13 (June 27, 1983), p. 60.

[29]   Brightman, Richard. *Information Systems for Modern Management*. New York: Macmillan, 1971.

[30]   Brooks, Frederick P. *The Mythical Man-Month*. Reading, Massachusetts: Addison-Wesley, 1975.

[31]   Brown, Gary D. and Donald H. Sefton. "The Micro vs. the Applications LogJam." *Datamation*, vol. 30, no. 1 (January 1984), pp. 96–104.

[32]   "Bumpy Road for Airline Stocks." *Wall Street Week*, No. 1508 (August 23, 1985).

[33]   Burch, John G. and Felix R. Strater. *Information Systems: Theory and Practice*. Santa Barbara, California: Hamilton Publishing Company, 1974.

[34]   Burch, John G., Felix R. Strater, and Gary Grudnitski. *Information Systems: Theory and Practice*, 2nd ed. New York: John Wiley & Sons, 1979.

[35]   "Business Takes a Second Look at Computers." *Business Week* (June 5, 1971), pp. 59–136.

[36]   Bylinsky, George. "Can Bell Labs Keep It Up?" *Fortune*, vol. 107, no. 13 (June 27, 1983), pp. 90–91.

[37]   Byrne, Richard. "Future Effects." *EDP Analyzer*, vol. 21, no. 11 (November 1983), pp. 7–9.

[38]   Campbell, Sullivan G. "Promises and Pitfalls." *Information Systems for Management*. Englewood Cliffs, New Jersey: Prentice-Hall, 1972, pp. 113–22.

[39]   Canning, E. G. *Guidelines for a Management Information System*. Vista, California: Canning Publications, 1965.

[40]   Carlson, Walter M. "Managing the Information Resource." *Chemical Engineering Progress*, vol. 68, no. 1 (January 1972), pp. 29–32.

[41]   Carpenter, C. E. "MIS Design Concepts." *Proceedings Third Annual Conference, Society for MIS, Denver, Colorado, September 1971*. Chicago: The Society for Management Information Systems, 1971.

[42]   "Changing Phone Habits." *Business Week* (September 5, 1983), pp. 68–76.

[43]   Clifton, H. D. *Systems Analysis for Business Data Processing*, rev. ed. New York: Petrocelli Books, 1974.

[44] Cobb, Richard H. "In Praise of 4GLs." *Datamation*, vol. 31, no. 14 (July 15, 1985), pp. 90-96.

[45] Coleman, Raymond J. and M. J. Riley. *Management Dimensions*. San Francisco: Holden-Day, 1973.

[46] "Computer for Repetitive Business Operations." *The Franklin Institute Journal*, vol. 266 (August 1985), pp. 148-49.

[47] "Computers Go To Work." *The Oil & Gas Journal* (July 21, 1958), p. 62.

[48] Condon, Robert J. *Data Processing Systems Analysis and Design*. Reston, Virginia: Reston Publishing Company, 1975.

[49] Costello, J. C. "Some Thoughts on the Information Problem." *Materials Research & Standards* (June 1961), pp. 474-6.

[50] Couger, J. Daniel. "Questions Yet Unresolved." *Computing Newsletter for Schools of Business*, vol. 16, no. 2 (October, 1982), p. 1.

[51] _____. "The Social Impact of Computers—From the System Designer Perspective." *Computing Newsletter for Schools of Business* vol. 16, no. 6 (February 1983), p. 1.

[52] _____. "Software Development Workbench." *Computing Newsletter for Schools of Business*, vol. 16, no. 6 (February 1983), p. 7.

[53] Couger, J. Daniel and Fred R. McFadden. *Introduction to Computer Based Information Systems*. New York: John Wiley & Wons, 1975.

[54] "Culture Shock Is Shaking the Bell System." *Business Week* (September 26, 1983), pp. 112-18.

[55] "Data Processing Equipment Needed Tomorrow." *SAE Journal*, vol. 71 (March 1963), pp. 58-62.

[56] "Data Processor Accepts Eight Programs Simultaneously." *Automation*, vol. 6 (May 1959), pp. 9-10.

[57] Davis, Gordon B. *Management Information Systems: Conceptual Foundations, Structure, and Development*. New York: McGraw-Hill, 1974.

[58] Dearden, John. "Can Management Information Be Automated?" *Harvard Business Review*, vol. 42, no. 2 (March-April 1964), pp. 128-35.

[59] Delbecq, Andre L., Andrew H. Van de Ven, and David H. Gustafson. *Group Techniques for Program Planning*. Glenview, Illinois: Scott Foresman & Company, 1975.

[60] DeMarco, Thomas. "Mystical Information Systems." *Information Systems for Management*. Englewood Cliffs, New Jersey: Prentice-Hall, 1972, pp. 9-12.

[61] Denise, Richard. "Technology for the Executive Thinker." *Datamation*, vol. 29, no. 6 (June 1983), pp. 206-17.

[62] Denison, Lea. "Arthur Andersen's Methodology for Systems Analysis." Unpublished paper written for credit in ISY 5V98 (April 23, 1985).

[63] Dickson, Gary W. "The Psychology of Systems Design: An Introduction." *Proceedings Sixth Annual Conference, Society for MIS, San Francisco, California, September 1974*. Chicago: The Society for Management Information Systems, 1976.

[64] Dippel, Gene and William C. House. *Information Systems: Data Processing and Evaluation*. Glenview, Illinois: Scott, Foresman & Company, 1969.

[65] Ebdon, J. F. "Trends for 1958: Increased Use of Computers." *Gas*, vol. 34 (January 1958), pp. 99-101.

[66] Eis, Shirley. "Evolution of the Information Center." *Infosystems*, vol. 32, no. 6 (June 1985), p. 41.

[67] Finke, W. W. "New Giant Brain for Businessmen." *The Franklin Institute Journal*, vol. 264 (December 1957), p. 456.

[68] Fioravanti, Janice. "AT&T Says It's Ready for Business, But Is Your Company Ready for AT&T?" *Data Communications Extra* (Mid-October 1984), pp. 29-38.

[69]   Flax, Steven. "The Orphan Called Baby Bell." *Fortune*, vol. 107, no. 13 (June 27, 1983), pp. 87–88.

[70]   "Fourth Generation Languages and Prototyping." *EDP Analyzer Special Report*. Vista, California: Canning Publications, 1984.

[71]   Frenkel, Karen A. "Toward Automating the Software-Development Cycle." *Communications of the ACM*, vol. 28, no. 6 (June 1985), pp. 578–89.

[72]   "G.E. 22:5 Information Processing System." *Control Engineering*, vol. 7 (July 1960), p. 22.

[73]   Gibson, Cyrus F. and Richard L. Nolan. "Managing the Four Stages of EDP Growth." *Harvard Business Review* (January–February 1974), pp. 76–88.

[74]   _____. "Organizational Issues in the Stages of EDP Growth." *Data Base*, vol. 5, nos. 2, 3, 4 (Winter 1973), pp. 50–68.

[75]   Gifford, David and Alfred Spector. "The TWA Reservation Systems." *Communications of the ACM*, vol. 27, no. 7 (July 1984), pp. 649–65.

[76]   Glaser, R. George. "Are You Working on the Right Problem?" *Datamation*, vol. 13, no. 8 (June 1967), p. 22.

[77]   Gore, Marvin and John Stubb. *Elements of Systems Analysis for Business Data Processing*. Dubuque, Iowa: Wm. C. Brown Publishers, 1975.

[78]   Grant, F. J. "The Downside of 4GLs." *Datamation*, vol. 31, no. 14 (July 15, 1985), pp. 99–104.

[79]   Gross, Paul and Robert D. Smith. *Systems Analysis and Design for Management*. New York: Dun-Donnelley Publishing Company, 1976.

[80]   Gruenberger, Fred. *Information Systems for Management*. Englewood Cliffs, New Jersey: Prentice-Hall, 1972.

[81]   Gurk, H. M. and J. Minker. "Design and Simulation of an Information Processing System." *Journal of the ACM*, vol. 8 (April 1961), pp. 260–70.

[82]   Halbrecht, Herbert Z. "The Future Manager of the Information Function – Industry's Changing Requirements." *Proceedings Seventh Annual Conference, Society for MIS, New York City, September 1975*. Chicago: The Society for Management Information Systems, 1976.

[83]   Hammerton, J. C. "Electronic Data Processing Systems for American Business." *Electronic Engineering*, vol. 32 (March 1960), pp. 148–54.

[84]   Hanson, Stephen J. and Richard R. Rosinski. "Programmer Perceptions of Productivity and Programming Tools." *Communications of the ACM*, vol. 28, no. 2 (February 1985), pp. 180–89.

[85]   Hargraves, Robert F., Jr. "Corporate Strategies and DP Tactics." *Datamation*, vol. 28, no. 8 (August 1983), pp. 204–16.

[86]   Harris, Byron. "The Man Who Killed Braniff." *Texas Monthly* (July 1982), pp. 116–20, 182–89.

[87]   Head, Robert B. *Manager's Guide to Management Information Systems*. Englewood Cliffs, New Jersey: Prentice-Hall, 1972.

[88]   Heany, Donald F. *Development of Information Systems*. New York: The Ronald Press Company, 1968.

[89]   Hicks, James O. *Management Information Systems: A User Perspective*. New York: West Publishing Company, 1984.

[90]   Hillhouse, Joseph: "The AT&T Divestiture: Now That the Cord's Been Cut." *Computer Decisions* (January 1984), pp. 180–82, 186–218.

[91]   Holmes, Edith. "Ma Bell and Her Seven Sisters." *Data Communications Extra* (Mid-October 1984), pp. 15–28.

[92]   _____. "Truth or Consequences: Can AT&T Deliver on Its Advertising Promises?" *Data Communications Extra* (Mid-October 1984), pp. 51–56.

[93]   Hume, W. S. "New Information Systems." *The Franklin Institute Journal*, vol. 272 (August 1961), pp. 160–61.

[94]   Hussain, Donna and K. M. Hussain. *Information Processing Systems for Management.* Homewood, Illinois: Richard D. Irwin, 1985.

[95]   Hutton, Thomas J. "Personal Computers: Management Tools or Executive Toys?" *Infosystems*, vol. 32, no. 6 (June 1985), pp. 96–97.

[96]   Ives, Blake and Gerard P. Learmonth. "The Information System As a Competitive Weapon." *Communications of The ACM*, vol. 27, no. 12 (December 1985), pp. 1193–1201.

[97]   Johnson, Floyd E. "Installing a Solution Center: Think Big, Start Small." *Infosystems*, vol. 32, no. 6 (June 1985), pp. 40–45.

[98]   Johnson, J. E. "Electronics to Start Revolution in Office." *The Franklin Institute Journal*, vol. 266 (May 1958), pp. 437–38.

[99]   _____. "Total Data Processing May Number Days of the Punched Card as a Business Document." *Gas Age*, vol. 121 (March 6, 1958).

[100]   Johnson, James R. "The Changing Data Processing Organization." *Datamation*, vol. 21, no. 1 (January 1975), pp. 81–83.

[101]   Johnson, Jan. "Strategies In the Services Realm." *Datamation*, vol. 28, no. 7 (July 1982), p. 47.

[102]   Johnson, Richard T. "The Infocenter Experience." *Datamation*, vol. 30, no. 1 (January 1984), pp. 137–42.

[103]   Kanter, Jerome. *Management Guide to Computer System Selection and Use.* Englewood Cliffs, New Jersey: Prentice-Hall, 1970.

[104]   Karasek, F. W. "Total Analysis Digital System for Chromatographs." *Analytical Chemistry*, vol. 33 (October 1961), pp. 1543–46.

[105]   Keen, Peter. "Managing Organizational Change: The Role of MIS." *Proceedings Seventh Annual Conference, Society for MIS, New York City, September 1975.* Chicago: The Society for Management Information Systems, 1976.

[106]   Keider, Stephen P. "Why Systems Development Projects Fail." *Journal of Information Systems Management*, vol. 1, no. 3 (Summer 1985), pp. 33–38.

[107]   Kelly, Joseph F. *Computerized Management Information Systems.* New York: Macmillan, 1970.

[108]   Kennevan, Walter J. "MIS Universe." *Data Management* (September 1970), p. 63.

[109]   King, David. *Current Practices in Software Development.* New York: Yourdon, 1984.

[110]   King, William R. and David I. Cleland. "The Design of Management Information Systems: An Information Analysis Approach." *Management Science*, vol. 22, no. 3 (November 1975), pp. 286–97.

[111]   Kling, Rob and Suzanne Iacono. "The Control of Information Systems Developments after Implementation." *Communications of The ACM*, vol. 27, no. 12 (December 1984), pp. 1218–26.

[112]   Knox, C. S. "Computer Simplifies Purchasing Decisions." *SAE Journal*, vol. 66 (July 1958), pp. 29–31.

[113]   Kornblum, B. L. "Let Information Retrieval Work for You." *Food Engineering*, vol. 35 (February 1963), pp. 45–47.

[114]   Krauss, Leonard I. *Computer Based Management Information Systems.* Chicago: American Management Association, 1970.

[115]   Lee, Alan F. "Why Prototyping Works." *Infosystems*, vol. 32, no. 3 (March 1985), pp. 88–89.

[116] Levine, S. "Fast-response Data Communication System for Airline Reservations." *Communications & Electronics*, vol. 599 (January 1963), pp. 599–600.

[117] Levine, S. and R. J. Buegler. "Large-scale Systems Engineering for Airline Reservations." *Electronic Engineering*, vol. 81 (August 1962), pp. 604–8.

[118] Levy, Joel D. "Bridging the Gap with Business Information Systems Planning." *Infosystems* (June 1982), pp. 82–84.

[119] Li, David H. *Design and Management of Information Systems*. Chicago: Science Research Associates, Inc., 1972.

[120] Loomis, Carol J. "Valuing the Pieces of Eight." *Fortune*, vol. 107, no. 13 (June 27, 1983), pp. 70–78.

[121] Lucas, Henry C., Jr. *The Analysis, Design and Implementation of Information Systems*. New York: McGraw-Hill, 1976.

[122] _____. *Computer Based Information Systems in Organizations*. Chicago: Science Research Associates, 1973.

[123] _____. *Toward Creative Systems Design*. New York: Columbia University Press, 1974.

[124] _____. *Why Information Systems Fail*. New York: Columbia University press, 1975.

[125] McCartney, Laton. "Breaking Up Is Hard to Do." *Datamation*, vol. 29, no. 8 (August 1983), pp. 36–45.

[126] McFarland, Warren. "Using the Computer as a Competitive Advantage." Speech to the Society for Information, Chicago, Illinois, October 1984.

[127] Mader, Chris. *Information Systems: Technology, Economics, Applications*. Chicago: Science Research Associates, 1972.

[128] Maynard, A. F. "Automation for Small-Lot Producers: Systems Approach." *Automation*, vol. 54 (March 1958), p. 8.

[129] Mellichamp, Joseph M. "MIS: Which Way to Go?" *Journal of Systems Management*, vol. 24, no. 7 (July 1973), pp. 34–37.

[130] Meredith, Denis C. "System Development Methodologies Provide Project Fire Power." *Data Management*, vol. 23, no. 8 (August 1985), pp. 22–24.

[131] Miles, Mary. "Information Management: Becoming A Specialist's Game?" *Computer Decisions*, vol. 16, no. 14 (November 1, 1984), pp. 158–69.

[132] Millar, Victor E. "Decision-oriented Information." *Datamation*, vol. 30, no. 1 (January 1984), pp. 159–62.

[133] Mitchell, E. W. "How to Get More from Your Data Processing System." *Iron Age*, vol. 121 (March 12, 1959), p. 3.

[134] Moss, James. "Planning a Management Information System." *Automation*, vol. 11 (August 1964), pp. 58–61.

[135] Murdick, Robert C. and Joel E. Ross. *Information Systems for Modern Management*. 1st ed. Englewood Cliffs, New Jersey: Prentice-Hall, 1971.

[136] _____. *Information Systems for Modern Management*. 2nd ed. Englewood Cliffs, New Jersey: Prentice-Hall, 1975.

[137] Murphy, Dennis J. "Defining Management's Needs Is Key to Designing Successful Management Information Systems." *Automation* (May 1969), pp. 74–74.

[138] "New Data Handling System: Kybernetes Data Handling." *Electronic Engineering*, vol. 32 (November 1960), p. 695.

[139] "New Gear Needed to Move the Literature Mountain." *Control Engineering*, vol. 8 (May 1961), p. 32.

[140] Nicholson, Charles H. "MIS in Perspective." *Chemical Engineering Progress*, vol. 66, no. 1 (January 1970), pp. 18–22.

[141]   Nolan, Richard L. "Managing the Crises in Data Processing." *Harvard Business Review*, vol. 57, no. 2 (March–April 1979), pp. 115–26.

[142]   Nolan, Richard L. and Henry H. Seward. "Measuring User Satisfaction to Evaluate Information Systems." *Administration: Systems Development.* Homewood, Illinois: Richard D. Irwin, Inc., 1971.

[143]   O'Connor, T. J. "Computer-Aided Parts Data Processing System." *Bell Labs Record*, vol. 41 (September 1963), pp. 294–302.

[144]   "Oil Industry Looks to Computers." *Electronics*, vol. 30 (December 1, 1957), p. 22.

[145]   Oliver, Paul. "Approaches to Software Engineering." *Journal of Information Systems Management* vol. 2, no. 3 (Summer 1985), pp. 11–19.

[146]   Optner, Stanford L. *Systems Analysis for Business Management.* 3rd ed. Englewood Cliffs, New Jersey: Prentice-Hall, 1975.

[147]   O'Reilly, Brian. "Ma Bell's Kids Fight for Position." *Fortune*, vol. 107, no. 13 (June 27, 1983), pp. 62–68.

[148]   Porter, Michael E. and Victor E. Millar. "How Information Gives You Competitive Advantage." *Harvard Business Review* (July–August 1985), pp. 149–60.

[149]   "Practical Retrieval System Developed." *Electronics*, vol. 32 (October 16, 1959), p. 88.

[150]   Prince, Thomas R. *Information Systems for Management Planning and Control.* Homewood, Illinois: Richard D. Irwin, Inc., 1966.

[151]   "Production Data Collection System." *Automation*, vol. 7 (December 1960), p. 54.

[152]   Radford, K. J. *Information Systems in Management.* Reston, Virginia: Reston Publishing Company, Inc., 1973.

[153]   Rae, Sharon G. "Application Generators: Cutting Back on Programmer Waste." *ICP Data Processing Management*, vol. 9, no. 1 (Spring 1984), pp. 34–36.

[154]   Rainbow, J. "Presently Available Tools for Information Retrieval." *Electronic Engineering*, vol. 77 (June 1958), pp. 494–98.

[155]   Reimann, Bernard C. and Allan D. Waren. "User-Oriented Criteria for the Selection of DSS Software." *Communications of the ACM*, vol. 28, no. 2 (February 1985), pp. 166–79.

[156]   Rhodes, Wayne L. "The Wake of Divestiture." *Infosystems*, vol. 32, no. 3 (March 1985), pp. 36–38.

[157]   Riley, D. L. "Information Retrieval: A Valuable Tool or Costly Waste?" *Journal of Petroleum Technology* (August 1963), p. 847.

[158]   Ringling, Fritz W. "AT&T: The UnBelled Underdog?" *Computer Decisions* (January 1985), pp. 102, 218–20.

[159]   Robinson, M. D. "Weyerhaeuser Approach to MIS, Introduction." *Proceedings Third Annual Conference, Society for MIS, Denver, Colorado, September 1971.* Chicago: The Society for Management Information Systems, 1971.

[160]   _____. "Weyerhaeuser Approach to MIS, Conclusion." *Proceedings Third Annual Conference, Society for MIS, Denver, Colorado, September 1971.* Chicago: The Society for Management Information Systems, 1971.

[161]   Roman, David. "MIS On the Attack." *Computer Decisions* (February 26, 1985), pp. 80–89.

[162]   Rosove, Perry E. *Developing Computer Based Information Systems.* New York: John Wiley & Sons, 1967.

[163]   Ross, Joel E. *Modern Management and Information Systems.* Reston, Virginia: Reston Publishing Company, 1976.

[164]   "SABRE Cuts Airline Reservation Time," *Electronic Engineering*, vol. 79 (January 1960), pp. 109–10.

[165]   Sanders, Donald H. *Computers and Management*. 1st ed. New York: McGraw-Hill, 1970.

[166]   _____. *Computers and Management*. 2nd ed. New York: McGraw-Hill, 1974.

[167]   _____. *Computers in Business*. New York: McGraw Hill, 1972.

[168]   Sapronov, Walter. "Deregulation and Telecommunications Acquisition." *Spectrum*, vol. 2, no. 4 (August 1985).

[169]   Schubert, E. J. "For Data Handling Systems, Printed Diode and Resistor Matrices." *Electronics Industry*, vol. 18 (December 1959), pp. 74–78.

[170]   Scott, George M. *Principles of Management Information Systems*. New York: McGraw-Hill, 1986.

[171]   Shaw, John C. and William Atkins. *Managing Computer System Projects*. New York: McGraw-Hill, 1970.

[172]   Shaw, R. F. "What's Available for Digital Data Transmission Control?" *Control Engineering*, vol. 8 (February 1961), pp. 127–33.

[173]   Showers, J. L. and L. M. Chakrin. "Reducing Uncollectible Revenue from Residential Telephone Customers." *Interfaces*, vol. 11, no. 6 (December 1981), pp. 21–34.

[174]   Silver, Gerald A. and Joan B. Silver. *Introduction to Systems Analysis*. Englewood Cliffs, New Jersey: Prentice-Hall, 1976.

[175]   Sisson, Roger. "Solution Systems and MIS." *Proceedings Twelfth Annual Conference, Society for MIS. September 1980.* Chicago: Society for Information Management Systems, 1980.

[176]   Smith, A. W. "How EDP Is Affecting Middle Management." *Administrative Managemente* (May 1966), pp. 42–48.

[177]   Smith, Peter M. "A Prototyping Case Study." *Journal of Information Systems Management*, vol. 2, no. 3 (Summer 1985), pp. 20–25.

[178]   Snyders, Jan. "The Benefits of Programmer Productivity Software." *Infosystems*, vol. 32, no. 6 (June 1985), pp. 59–64.

[179]   _____. "Generators Do the Trick." *Computer Decisions* (June 1982), pp. 210–26.

[180]   Southwestern Bell Telephone Company. *Universal Service Order Practice, Southwestern Bell Telephone Company.* St. Louis, Missouri: Southwestern Bell Telephone Company Intracompany Publications, 1973.

[181]   Stallings, William. "Beyond Local Networks." *Datamation*, vol. 29, no. 8 (August 1983), pp. 167–80.

[182]   Steiner, George A. *Top Management Planning*. Toronto, Canada: Collier-Macmillan Canada, 1969.

[183]   Stix, Gary. "Telecomm: What Hath Been Wrought?" *Computer Decisions*, vol. 17, no. 1 (January 15, 1985), pp. 96–101.

[184]   Tharrington, James M. "The Science of MIS Planning." *Infosystems*, vol. 32, no. 6 (June 1985), pp. 52–54.

[185]   Thayer, G. N. "BIS in the Bell System." *Bell Labs Record* (December 1968), pp. 354–61.

[186]   Thierauf, Robert J. *Systems Analysis and Design of Real Time Management Information Systems*. Englewood Cliffs, New Jersey: Prentice-Hall, 1975.

[187]   Thomas, D. E., Jr. "Making Management Information Systems Work." *Automation* (November 1971), pp. 30–33.

[188]   Tolliver, Edward. "Myths of Automated Management Systems." *Journal of Systems Management* (March 1971), pp. 29–32.

[189]   Tomeski, Edward A. "A Blueprint for Master Planning of MIS." *Management Information Systems*. Cleveland, Ohio: Association for Systems Management, 1974, pp. 48–53.

[190] "Total MIS: How It Is Achieved." *Canadian Chemical Processing* (October 1964), p. 80.

[191] Uttal, Bro. "Western Electric's Cold New World." *Fortune*, vol. 107, no. 13 (June 27, 1983), pp. 80–84.

[192] Vacca, John R. "The Information Center's Critical Post-Startup Phase." *Journal of Information Systems Management*, vol. 2, no. 2 (Spring 1985), pp. 50–56.

[193] Waggener, Robert C. "Restoring Systems' Tarnished Charisma." *Journal of Systems Management* (September 1974), pp. 22–24.

[194] Ware, Thomas M. "Keynote Address: Management Communications." *Proceedings Seventh Annual Conference, Society for MIS, New York City, September 1975*. Chicago: The Society for Management Information Systems, 1976.

[195] Watson, Hugh J. and Archie B. Carroll. *Computers for Business: A Managerial Emphasis*. Dallas, Texas: Business Publications, 1976.

[196] Weber, May. "A Psychoanalytic Approach to MIS." *Proceedings Sixth Annual Conference, Society for MIS, San Francisco, California, September 1974*. Chicago: The Society for Management Information Systems, 1976.

[197] Weinberg, Gerald M. and Daniela Weinberg. "What Do Users Really Want? Part I: The 30-Minute Expert." *Journal of Information Systems Management*, vol. 2, no. 2 (Spring 1985), pp. 68–71.

[198] Weir, J. M. "Bell System Data Processing Today." *Bell Labs Record*, vol. 39 (October 1961), pp. 359–61.

[199] Wetherbe, James C. and Robert L. Leitheiser. "Information Centers: A Survey of Services, Decisions, Problems, and Successes." *Journal of Information Systems Management,* vol. 2, no. 3 (Summer 1985), pp. 3–10.

[200] "What Computers Can and Cannot Do." *Canadian Chemical Processing*, vol. 42 (March 1985), pp. 103–6.

[201] "Where the 'User-Friendly' Concept Began." *Business Week* (March 28, 1983), p. 54.

[202] Withington, Frederick G. "Five Generations of Computers." *Harvard Business Review* (March–April 1974), pp. 99–108.

[203] _____. "Sizing Each Other Up." *Datamation*, vol. 28, no. 7 (July 1982), pp. 8–23.

[204] _____. "Will Technology Save the Day?" *Information Systems for Management*. Englewood Cliffs, New Jersey: Prentice-Hall, 1972, pp. 89–96.

[205] Woodford, Donald R. "BIS." *Bell Telephone Magazine* (December 1961), pp. 2–10.

[206] Wrigley, Bruce H. "From the Chairman." *Proceedings of the Wharton Conference on Research on Computers in Organizations*. Special Report No. 2 (December 1973), p. i.

[207] Yingling, John E., Jr. "Planning for BIS Installation." *Bell Labs Record* (June/July 1972), pp. 189–93.

[208] Young, Lawrence F. "Hiring Qualified College Graduates: MIS Business Majors versus Computer Science Majors." *Journal of Information Systems Management*, vol. 2, no. 3 (Summer 1985), pp. 70–72.

[209] Zani, William M. "Blueprint for MIS." *Harvard Business Review* (December 1970), pp. 95–100.

[210] Zvegintzov, Nicholas. "Nanotrends." *Datamation*, vol. 29, no. 8 (August 1983), pp. 106–16.

Interviews

[211] Hooper, Max. Personal interview held at Tulsa, Oklahoma, August 1976.

[212] Toma, C. E. Personal interview held at Tulsa, Oklahoma, August 1976.

[213]   Weyerhaeuser Corporation. Personal interview with company representative held at Tacoma, Washington, August 1976.

Index